NO

SMOKE

WITHOUT

FIRE

A recipe for disaster

Brian B Humphreys

To

George and Violet

No Smoke Without Fire
Copyright © 2019 by Brian B Humphreys

Photo Credit:
Front and Back Cover by: Randy Whitbread

Credit to Editor: Rick Johnson

Tellwell Talent
www.tellwell.ca

ISBN
978-0-2288-2297-4 (Hardcover)
978-0-2288-2295-0 (Paperback)
978-0-2288-2296-7 (eBook)

This book is dedicated to all the people of Flin Flon who were affected by the disastrous smelter explosion Aug. 8, 2000, to the many workers on the Hudson Bay Mining Fatality List included near the end of the book, and to all workers who lose their lives at work every year.

Acknowledgements

It would be remiss of me not to acknowledge the appreciation I hold for the companies for which I have spent a lifetime working – the British Steel Corporation, Shotton Works in Deeside North Wales, and Hudson Bay Mining and Smelting in Flin Flon, Manitoba.

I consider myself very fortunate to have had the opportunity to be part of both their workforces. As a result, I have met and worked with some truly remarkable people.

The bravery of the employees who were severely injured in the Flin Flon explosion Aug. 8, 2000, is also acknowledged. The care and attention given them by their fellow workmates was incredible and heroic.

I also acknowledge the ambulance attendants, HBM&S fire department and Plant Protection officers, staff of the Flin Flon General Hospital, and all emergency services used that evening. No amount of training or practice could ever prepare someone for the disaster those people faced.

I must also acknowledge the HBM&S Mine Rescue and Fire Department emergency crews involved in retrieving accident victims. It is only in the last 20-odd years that the impact of post-traumatic stress upon such rescue workers and co-workers has been truly recognized. Also the

United Steelworkers USW 7106 for their compilation and distribution of the HBM&S fatality list that has been used in this book.

Larry Scully, who, unfortunately, is no longer with us, gave me the strength and guidance to carry on when I needed to in the dark days that followed that horrendous event. As well, acknowledgement and appreciation are offered to my daughters, Samantha and Colette, Son in Law Dennis McDermott, for their love and support. They had to witness the anguish and despair that I could not escape after the tragedy.

And I offer my deeply felt thanks to the many people who have helped and supported me in the writing of this book: my editor, Rick Johnson, Tellwell Publishers, Randy Whitbread for his cover photographs, my sister Janet Share and husband Mick, Max Ferrier, Perry and Trudy Burton, Tony Pickering, and Al Mccarthy, to name just a few.

Most especially, I acknowledge and thank my life partner, Helen. Throughout this journey, she has always shown me unwavering support, often holding me together when I could so easily have fallen apart.

Table of Contents

Foreword

Preface

A total of 14 workers, 12 employed by Hudson Bay Mining and Smelting, and two by contractors, sustained physical injuries Aug. 8, 2000, in the smelter explosion in Flin Flon, Manitoba. Injuries requiring hospitalization included severe burns, lung damage, eye injuries and dust inhalation. After receiving first aid on site, seven employees were hospitalized while seven others were treated and released.

Four employees in critical condition were taken by air ambulance to burn units in Winnipeg, Regina, and Edmonton. Another worker was later transported to a hospital in Winnipeg. Tragically, the explosion claimed the life of one employee, who died eight days later from the horrific burns he had received.

So why on earth, 19 years after one of the worst mining disasters in Manitoba, does somebody want to write a book about it. Truth be told, as one of the two safety supervisors on shift when the explosion occurred, I started the book as therapy a short time afterwards. As part of my post-traumatic stress counselling, I was advised to capture my feelings by writing them down. And, indeed, putting my thoughts on paper helped me in my efforts to make some sense of it all, to understand how and why such a tragedy could ever have taken place.

Having left the furnace only a few minutes prior to the explosion, the event had a profound effect on me… and still does! The immediate aftermath was likened to a war zone. If you can visualize what looking into hell might be like, I am sure what I saw that day would be pretty close.

So, this writing began, not with the intent of writing a book, but as a form of release to ease my mind and to try to find some solace after what had taken place.

After a lengthy government investigation, which concluded on Oct. 4, 2000, nine recommendations for changes in operating procedures during a smelter shutdown and rebuild were made to Hudson Bay Mining and Smelting. Those changes included allowing an adequate cooling period after the burners had been shut off; restricting the use of water in the reverberatory furnace; ensuring that exits from the smelter are not locked or blocked; investigating alternative means, other than water, for cleaning calcine buildup in the hoppers and dust from the calcine floor, beams and furnace arch.

The government investigation team included the chief occupational medical officer, two mining engineers, one civil engineer, one engineer with a PhD in metallurgy, two certified occupational hygienists, two safety and health officers, one mines inspector, and one special projects officer.

Three consultants were also hired: a metallurgist and mechanical engineer; a metallurgical engineer, and a professor of chemistry. The investigation team examined and sampled the explosion site, reviewed operating records and conducted 46 interviews of people involved in the smelter operations.

The 710-page report was forwarded to Manitoba Justice for review to determine if there were grounds for prosecution under the Workplace Safety and Health Act.

The company pleaded guilty to having an unsafe workplace in connection with the explosion and was fined $150,000. Many would consider that a pittance compared to what it should have been. When you add up the cost of the incident in terms of human suffering, loss of production, and damage to the reputation of a company that had prided itself on safety, no amount of money could have adequately compensated.

Other measures taken included changes to regulations, training and risk assessments, and written safe-work procedures to prevent similar events from ever happening again. Yet, still something seemed to be missing.

My work history spans over 49 years in heavy industry. I spent 13 years in steelmaking in Wales before moving to Canada and a total of 36 years in the Flin Flon mining industry. I was a health and safety co-ordinator at the mine for 28 years prior to my retirement. I felt that when I retired, I could share some of my experiences with workers, supervisors and managers in the hope that by gaining more insight into why and how people lose their lives on the job, similar events might be prevented.

Examples given and discussions throughout this book are not intended to demean or point a finger at any individual, group or company. They are purely used as learning opportunities to help people recognize and understand that sometimes it is only by incredible luck or good fortune that they don't end up seriously injured, or even killed.

The examples are mostly centred around heavy industry, but many similar occurrences lay dormant in all workplaces, and even outside the work environment.

Flin Flon is a small town nestled in the Precambrian Shield, otherwise known as Greenstone. People living in the area were used to seeing smoke oozing out of the smelter's 825-foot stack, the second largest in Canada. It remains a landmark that can be seen for miles, and often a welcome sight to the weary traveller. The smoke itself was never a good thing, but it did represent the lifeblood of the community.

When the furnace was shut down on Aug. 7, 2000, for a major rebuild that was expected to last just 10 days, nobody dreamed they would not see smoke from that stack again for almost two months. The horrific events that took place on that fateful evening will forever remain in the minds of workers, families, and friends.

To reiterate, this book it is not about blame or finger pointing. It is an attempt to capture and understand the circumstances that led up to the explosion and what goes into a recipe for such a disaster. When you sprinkle a little of this and a little of that into a recipe you invariably end up with something. Seldom is anything made from one ingredient. Similarly, a disaster is usually triggered by more than one single event or "ingredient."

I
THE
INGREDIENTS

Flin Flon

Flin Flon was born of mining and mining remains its sustenance. Like a perpetual motion machine, its power and energy feed from within.

In fact, it is one of the most interesting and unique facts about this city that its original purpose for being still exists 90 years after its inception. Most cities start off with some purpose, of course, but as time goes by, they grow and change and their original reason for being is forgotten or becomes obsolete. Flin Flon, however, still retains its original purpose and proud record of mining copper, gold, zinc and other precious metals.

The city was never really meant to last as long as it has. The early prospectors came and set up tents for shelter over the first harsh winters. The mineral resources that were found always seemed to have a five to 10-year life span. Early deposits were easier to mine; the open pit was one such deposit. Mine equipment and machinery was limited and the work was more physically demanding. Tonnages were slower to retrieve and took more manpower.

When you compare some of the earlier deposits mined and the time it took to mine them out, today's modern equipment and mining methods would have depleted the reserves in next to no time at all.

With the mine being the sole reason for the town's existence and, by far, its lifeblood, the local economy has been held in its grip. That grip always tightened during contract negotiation years, but it was not as though the workforce was particularly militant. In fact, only once in the history of the company have workers exercised their right to strike.

However, there were enough people around during subsequent contract years who had experienced the strike that the term "possible strike" was never too far away in many conversations.

The negotiation process was, and still is, a drawn-out affair that also affects local business. Building permits taken out in a contract year are a rarity that only an optimist or a fool might consider. Many a good local business did not survive contract years.

On the other hand, the mine was a good provider, it was not solely dependent on only one mineral. It seemed that whenever one of its commodities slipped in value another one increased to compensate.

Wages earned at the mine were steady. In fact, if you were looking for a definition of a steady pay cheque you might find it in a mining job in Flin Flon. With few forced layoffs and a high turnover of labour in the earlier years, a job at the company meant something.

The legacy of this ever-shrinking community is one of pride and commitment, a lasting tribute to the pioneer days of hard work, dedication and spirit. Nobody wants to be the one who pulls the plug when the city's resources are depleted, and its lifeblood is drained.

More and more, the local population looks further afield to purchase the niceties of life. Stores such as The Bay, Eaton's, and Woolworth's have closed, leaving a skeleton of what once was a thriving local economy. Prince Albert and Saskatoon, Saskatchewan, have reaped the benefits.

Still, Flinty, the cartoon caricature of the city, greets all visitors traveling into the city from the northeast, heralding the community as the only city in the world named after a fictional cartoon character. Some say only two highways lead to the "Sunless City" – one road in, and one road out! Apart from those two roads, the rail line, airport, and a smaller airstrip are its only links to the outside. But the community seems almost oblivious to the outside world, and its geographical location would appear to confirm the wisdom in that.

Anyone who has not grown up in a small, isolated community may not fully understand the feeling that exists in one. Something similar may well exist in a large metropolis if you consider a subdivision as having a separate identity from the rest of a major urban centre. A suburb might attract and take on certain characteristics that do not exist in the rest of the city but, still, that is different than being an isolated community.

Try to imagine what it would be like to have your suburb, the neighbourhood in which you live, transported to an isolated area a four-hour drive away from the rest of your city.

What small isolated communities provide is unique and can only be realized by experiencing the close interaction of people, which extends to all parts of life: recreation, community, education, worship, and work. You would be hard pressed while living in such a community to walk into a coffee shop, the local legion, a doctor's office, or a store without being recognized, and recognizing others.

Now, curling clubs struggle to hold onto their precious memberships. Service clubs, too, compete to survive as the population shrinks ever smaller. It's a viscous circle not readily noticeable, but when you take a step back and look at a period of, say 10 years, hard reality begins to set in.

So, what has all this to do with one of the worst industrial accidents that Manitoba has seen in years? The city has shrunk considerably over the years. It is a "city" in legal terms only. It is really a small, isolated community that breeds a particular familiarity that makes such a disaster even worse.

The Company

It is sad to say, but most people refer to their employer as just "The Company!" Seldom, if ever, do they say, "our company." This lack of personal ownership in the life blood of a community is unfortunate, and disturbing.

Having been passed down over many years this would be almost impossible to change… unless all employees were shareholders! They are obvious stakeholders, but seldom see themselves as such, let alone as shareholders.

The company – our company – was owned by Anglo American Corporation and was slated for closure in 2004. However, an initiative that started in 1997 led to labour agreements and financial commitments that gave the mine and the surrounding area a future to 2016 and beyond.

In order to secure the large amount of money required to invest in new mines and processing something had to change. For a company that had not had a good profit-margin or safety track record in the years prior to securing the necessary loans, doing so was a remarkable achievement. Being in the last quartile of zinc producers worldwide, how do you get the necessary confidence from shareholders to dig deeper into their wallets?

Never is anyone at their best more than when they are threatened with extinction. In order to free up the millions of dollars it was going to require to keep the operation viable, everyone had to pull together. The two years prior to the disaster saw a concerted effort to keep Flin Flon on the map. For that, credit goes to the leadership of the company, the unions, the community, and the government of the day.

The company's books were laid open and the unions were invited to scrutinize them with whatever accounting expertise they could muster. They took up the challenge and learned that the company officers were not bluffing when they had said they were in trouble and that closure in 2004 was imminent.

A consulting group was hired, employee work groups were formed into business units and information on the business was made readily available. Project feasibility studies were undertaken, and safety became front and centre, being included as an agenda item at all meetings.

During that time, confidence began to grow, the company's performance began to match its shareholders expectations and accident frequency rates began to tumble to the best in history.

The company and the unions reached an unprecedented no-strike, no-lockout labour agreement that would last until 2012, contingent on a multi-million-dollar investment. In order to become more efficient and be able to compete in the new global economy, manpower reductions became inevitable and were achieved through opening pension windows to more senior employees in the form of no penalty reductions in pensions for early retirees.

The downside to this initiative was that senior employees were experienced employees. You cannot substitute experience and knowledge with anything else – another ingredient in the recipe for disaster!

Most employees were looking forward to the new challenges that a shutdown brings, a break from their normal routine, a chance to learn new skills and an opportunity to make some extra money through overtime.

New methods and equipment were going to be used to reduce the heavy physical labour that was traditional with the shutdowns that had occurred before.

A D7 Cat, a large bulldozer on caterpillar tracks, was to replace the skidder for furnace brick removal. Remote controlled "Brokk" machines would replace men on jackhammers. There was an air of optimism.

The People

The people of Flin Flon are a hardy, mostly friendly bunch, typical of what you would expect to find in any small, isolated northern community.

Around the mine everyone has a nickname: The Godfather, Little Louie, Skid, Pic, Smoke, Dr. Evil, Stinger, Mr. Potato Head, Fingers, Haystack, and Moose Lumpy, Tar, Stretch, Popa Kraz, Super Dave, Black Bob, Whitey,. Some enjoy the notoriety their nickname gives them; some are unaware they have one because it is only used to refer to them when they are not present.

Many are now second and third generation residents. Many were born here of parents who came to seek some stability in the depression and war years. Some who were born and raised in Flin Flon broke loose in search of greener pastures only to eventually find themselves back in the shadow of the smokestack. They are the migrant workers who drift in and out following the work when it is aplenty and staying only a short while when it is not.

Employees who have served a trade apprenticeship at the company are revered as among the best. The experience of learning their craft in a fully integrated copper and zinc producing environment that has everything from

60-year-old technology to today's technological marvels is hard to emulate. They have learned to react quickly and efficiently under pressure and pride themselves in keeping things going, considering the mine's geographical location.

Having the operation shut down for an extended period while waiting for a shipment of a critical component to arrive on-site was never an option. Using their skills and ingenuity, pattern makers, foundry workers, machinists, carpenters, motor winders, electricians, and boilermaker welders could literally manufacture, build or repair anything that was required to keep the operation going.

Unfortunately, apprenticeships are affected by depressed economic times when metal prices are low, their numbers dwindling to single digits that are swallowed up in a workforce of 1,500. It is said that men only fully mature when they are in a position to teach and train younger men. With little to no apprentices coming through the system, a man's knowledge becomes stifled, not getting the opportunity to pass on the tricks of the trade while, at the same time, reinforcing lessons learned from past masters.

As well, less desirable work locations, such as the smelter, have had their employees lured away by higher paying jobs underground, or better working conditions in other surface operations. It seems that whenever the smelter has finally invested the time and resources in their personnel to reach a level of proficiency, those workers leave, to be replaced by yet more greenhorns.

The trap that many employees fall into is that they get to a stage in their careers where, although they are not happy and would like a move, they stay because their seniority gives them more holidays each year, better choices, when choices are available, and an improved pension. They show up for work and put in time, but they are angry and vocal, the first to criticize and, although a minority, they have a negative effect on the rest of the workforce.

These disgruntled workers influence younger, newer employees, have little or no respect for supervisors or management, and look only to the day a pension window will open and they will be allowed to leave without penalty. They also stay because they realize they could never survive employment with a smaller company. Nor would a smaller company hire them.

When the average age of the workforce exceeds 40-plus and 10 percent are just putting in time, you have a problem on your hands. With enough seniority and a lack of discipline, some of the 10 percent believe they are bullet proof and can't be fired.

Fewer and fewer apprentices coming through the system, and discontented, unhappy workers not creating a climate for excellence, are hard realities, part of the recipe for disaster, and play an important role in creating the culture of a company.

Yet another factor, which most employees share and agree upon, is an intense dislike of contractors. They see their own numbers decreasing while there is an increase in on-site contractors and off-site contracting out. They view most contractors with suspicion because they take away their work and use their tools and equipment. Contractors take chances, work longer hours, and don't spend their pay cheques in the community, hence do nothing to boost the local economy.

However, truth be told, contractors are a necessary evil, when major projects are in progress. Their numbers and specialties are a necessity.

The Workers

The Good, the Bad and the Ugly!

Whenever you put a large number (1500) of individuals and personalities together you are going to get this mix. Fortunately, about 80 percent are good, 15 percent are bad, and five percent are ugly.

Human resource departments usually deal with 20 percent of the workforce when it comes to issues such as absenteeism, discipline, etc. With a little coaching and effort from the employer and employees in the 15 percent group, they could become good employees.

Let's start with the good, or should I say the great, the talented, and whatever other positive adjective you can use to describe dedicated, hard-working, and loyal employees. They are the type of people that if you owned your own company you would want to employ them. They truly care about the impact they can have on the profit line and profitable resources. They are not confined to the board room, although they can be found in abundance at that level and within all levels of an organization.

Small mining communities can easily fade into obscurity without good workers at all levels and sufficient attention to that profit line, and there are numerous examples: Lynn Lake, Elliot Lake, and Uranium City, to name a few.

Most company executives don't have to worry about making what is, for most people, their biggest purchase and investment, their home, because in many cases it is provided by their employer. You have to give a lot of credit to members of the regular workforce who risk losing their home and job at the same time in the event of a total mine closure.

The bad! They lack loyalty, commitment and skill. Unhappy with their daily work routine, they lack the vision to move ahead and make the best of the situation in which they find themselves. They have learned that if they complain hard and long enough, they can get changes made. However, just as one issue is resolved another materializes. There is always something for them to complain about. They never see themselves as being part of any solution. Their role is to identify problems, not solutions.

Then there are the Ugly! These people may not have started out in this category, and they make up only a very small percentage of the work force, but they are like a cancer. The bad feed from them. They lack conscience and truly don't give a damn if the company is successful or fails. Any new initiatives are treated with scorn, skepticism and condemnation. They hide behind and are reluctantly protected by their unions.

The British Invasion

The transient nature of the population in small mining towns and the need to have a certain number of trained employees was quite evident in 1980. The company experienced a severe shortage of trades personnel. The apprenticeship program called for a sufficient ratio of tradesmen to train apprentices but even advertising for three months across Canada did not make a dent in the need.

HBMS received permission to go overseas to fill the void, advertising in the British press for industrial mechanics, electricians, carpenters, and boilermaker welders. There was no shortage of applicants with over 3,000 putting their names forward. This reflected the state of some of the British industries at the time and the high unemployment rates in some British communities.

Seventy-six British families were relocated to Flin Flon from the UK within a year. A two-year contract covered moving and air travel expenses. However, by 1984 less than 10 families from the UK invasion still called Flin Flon home. That was quite remarkable when you consider that the company had received 3,000 applications for open positions and had carried out 100 interviews in each of the major industrial centres of London, Birmingham and Edinburgh. But all the time and effort spent on recruitment could not be sustained through follow-up nurturing and development.

Within two years, the company experienced a change in fortune and even reduced the trade requirements of its workforce. The majority of the 76 families took the opportunity to seek greener pastures, without penalty.

High turnover within the company at that time was a result of many issues and broken promises. The Brits were never told that their pre-existing trade credentials were not recognized in Canada and that they would have to write interprovincial Red Seal exams. They were given a six-month grace period to become certified or they would face a reduction in pay. Most of the new recruits had no difficulty acing the exams, but they were a little sour about not being told about them during the interview process.

The remoteness of Flin Flon, the long hard winters of sub-zero temperatures, lack of amenities that are sometimes taken for granted in larger urban centres, and mosquitos helped to deter families from staying. The mosquitos seemed particularly attracted to European blood.

Most Flin Flon residents welcomed the British invasion. Some were slightly amused at all the different accents that arrived on their doorsteps. Some said the newcomers talked like characters on Coronation Street. It was even said that one of the recruits from Glasgow was so hard to understand that even his wife struggled to comprehend him. Some Brits just never fit into the community, in part because they tended to stick together.

Friday nights in Branch 73 of the Royal Canadian Legion was meet-and-greet night for the new arrivals from across the pond. It was good to see the place packed and many a good night was had by all.

A shortage of good rental accommodation at the time meant many of the newcomers were housed in the newly built Green Street and Adams Street apartments. If they had previously lived in their own homes before they left the UK, moving into an apartment building was a traumatic experience for them, particularly if they had young children who were used to playing in a backyard.

Thank heaven for places like Phantom Lake, which offered a beach, concession and playground. Unfortunately, it only offered respite during the summer months. Living in the apartments in the winter took its toll on many of the British families, particularly those with small children.

Some of the Brits bought houses in the community but with mortgage rates running at over 20 percent at the time, it was sometimes hard to figure out if they were being brave or foolish.

All that paled in comparison to immigrants and refugees that come to Canada fleeing countries around the world where they had suffered persecution, starvation and the ravages of war. Many, owning nothing but the ragged clothes on their backs, came to escape, with the hope of a better life. The Brits came to further enrich their lives in, no doubt, one of the best and most compassionate countries on the planet.

As with all new people joining a company, they brought their experiences with them, along with some of their expectations about what they anticipated seeing in the workplace. It is fair to say that some were quite outspoken on some of the things they encountered that did not meet those expectations.

The safety culture or system at the time consisted largely of the slogan, "Tom Thumb says thumbs up for safety." It was plastered on posters, aired in radio announcements, and stickers were placed throughout the work areas, but nobody really knew what it was all about. Just having a jingle won't make workplaces safer. You have to have a safety program that identifies hazards and risks within a workplace and puts the necessary controls and other measures in place to reduce risk to an acceptable level.

One of the Brits was appalled when he saw another mechanic release the air from the braking system of a locomotive parked in the workshop waiting for maintenance. This was common practice but the quality of air in those tanks is not good, containing droplets of oil and moisture with antifreeze to prevent the airlines from freezing up in winter, not to mention a host of other likely contaminates.

The air in the workshop was noticeably different for quite some time after the air tanks had been drained. But how do you get a locomotive into the workshop with empty air tanks when the braking system is automatically applied when the tanks are empty? And you need the tanks to be empty when you work on a locomotive.

The Brit who questioned the practice also provided the solution. He had an airline pipe put through the wall of the shop to the outside of the building and lined it up to where the locomotive was parked inside. Whenever tanks needed to be drained, the line was hooked up to the valve on the tank and the exhausted air would be vented outside the building instead of inside.

It's always better to be part of the solution than part of the problem. This was just one of the many safety improvements made during that time, but it was certainly not a one-way street when it came to learning new ways of working. The Brits also learned a lot from the local tradesmen. Many were highly skilled in tasks that the British tradesman had never been exposed to.

Rigging was one of the areas of expertise in which the Canadian counterparts shone. Using cable, tuggers, and snatch blocks, it was simply amazing to watch them work their magic.

One example was when the ridding rings on one of the main dryers needed to be replaced. Ridding rings are two bands of steel that go around the cylindrical drum of a dryer. The dryer was a huge rotating drum with a furnace at one end.

The riggers would shimmy up the building's support structures and hang cables from the steel roof rafters. Next they would figure out if they needed a double or triple block, the correct angles, the size of tugger, and its precise location. They could manipulate the huge steel sections of ridding ring wherever they wanted to in the building. Removing the old and replacing with new rings with a flow of movement that resembled an orchestra in full swing.

No overhead crane existed in the building, yet everything was done with such precision and care. The crew always looked out for each other, like coaching the newbies not to stand in certain areas of the building should something go wrong, A cable break could decapitate or take your legs off if you didn't follow their advice.

In today's safety culture, I am not sure where you would even begin to perform the same work. Everything would have to be engineered, a safe-work plan developed, fall-arrest equipment used, etc. The list would go on and on.

These guys did everything without the need for anything other than their experience and imagination. In today's safety culture, workers are not expected to anticipate the hazards of the work they perform. Legislation demands that it is the owner's responsibility so it's the supervisor who carries that tremendous burden.

Crew meetings at the start of a shift usually consisted of a one-way conversation in which the supervisor doled out work assignments for the day. It very quickly became noticeable that anyone raising an issue or safety concern ended up with the worst job, or worst work location the following day.

One member of the British invasion, who was well known for his vocal expressions of concern, was finally broken. He was put on permanent nights and started each shift with a list of work assignments that could choke a horse.

Another employee volunteered to take his place on the night shift to give him a break and he, too, was put on nights as well. One night, the outspoken Brit came onto the night shift to find yet another list of assignments that could never be completed by a full crew, let alone one man.

"That's it! I quit!" he wrote in the shift log for that evening, and then walked out the gate never to return! In today's world, he would probably have had good grounds to file a harassment case. It was a far cry from today's crew meetings where employees are encouraged to discuss all their safety concerns and get them resolved ahead of time.

PASS (positive attitude safety system) and "Take Five" are all vehicles designed to improve overall safety and communication regarding hazards and concerns.

The Practice of Bumping

The practice of more senior employees moving into areas of the plant where they replace junior employees strikes at the very core of the union movement. Seniority of membership rules above all else.

It is one of the most difficult issues to deal with because it is hard to argue that someone who has been employed by the company for 10 years should lose his job to another employee who may have only worked for the company for two years.

Bumping takes place when new technology creates an opportunity to reduce manpower within a department, or mines close either temporarily or permanently.

The result is usually the same. An influx of more senior employees, with no experience of the new department, are parachuted in and force the exit of more junior but trained employees.

The smelter is particularly vulnerable to bumping. As one of the least desirable departments to work in, it holds a plentiful supply of junior employees. New employees who have been hired off the street are made aware that their positions are fragile and that likely they will be replaced when new technologies come online.

This practice is hardly conducive to encouraging junior employees to be the best that they can be and absorb all the training and finer points of the tasks they are assigned. How attentive they are, or how proficient they become does not count. Seniority rules, so they enter the workforce with one foot already out the door.

The Buddy System

One of the most-used ways to train new or transferred employees is the buddy system. The employee-in-training is placed with a more experienced employee while learning the job. This process relies heavily on the integrity not only of the more experienced worker to cover what he has learned, but also implies that he was given the correct procedures in the first place.

The buddy system can be very effective and work well if the person doing the training is motivated to do a good job of it. Some people are natural trainers and enjoy the experience of passing on their knowledge to younger employees (greenhorns). Others either do not feel qualified to train, lack good communication skills, or do not feel it is their responsibility to train people.

They may also be asked to train a more senior employee from another department, who, they fear, could ultimately bump them out of a job, which does not make for a good buddy relationship.

Well written procedures are fundamental to ensure that training requirements and knowledge transfers are fully met. The new job incumbent must also be able to demonstrate his newly acquired skills to his supervisor.

The Bonus System

Another detriment to smelter operations was the tremendous loss of experience created by the mine bonus system. The mine department has many bonuses, which are the key to their fortunes. It is one of the few areas within the company where employees can earn far more than their base rate of pay without having to work extraordinary amounts of overtime. Many experienced miners can make six figure wages.

It is seldom, if ever, that an employee is fortunate enough to get hired permanently straight into the mine department unless, that is, he is already skilled for the position available.

Most first enter the smelter workforce, not usually through choice, but rather out of necessity. It is a foot in the door. They will have to hope and be patient while they build up enough seniority to take an apprenticeship or a position in another area of the plant or mine. The No. 1 choice is the mine department and its bonus system. The smelter workforce is, therefore, extremely vulnerable in three ways.

The first is the bumping of junior employees by more senior ones who are being displaced from other areas of the plant due to technological change. The second is through transfers of smelter employees with seniority to more lucrative areas, such as the mine department. And, finally, smelter employees with experience leave because they finally qualify for early retirement.

All three ways offer some degree of hope, a light at the end of the tunnel. When you are wearing a respirator for eight to 12 hours a day, you need to know there is a means to a more desirable end.

How do you fix the problem? Not easy! It's sometimes easy to sit back and be critical of the company or the unions for the personnel problems that occur but the fix must come from within. Employees need to be rewarded for their efforts, not necessarily in monitory ways, but it certainly would help. When such large disparities are created the grass will always appear greener on the other side.

The Contractors

If there is one topic that unites the workforce, it is the general dislike of contractors and what they stand for. Contractors represent a loss of opportunity for regular workers, either through increasing contractor numbers, or through loss of overtime for the regular workforce.

They also represent a significant financial loss to small communities because they come only to work, not to spend! Most of their hard-earned cash is shipped back to their home bases. The only local benefactors are the local bars and hotels.

Contractors do work hard and put in long hours because it is better to be on-site making double time than to be stuck in their dorm or hotel room waiting for the start of their next shift. For the same reason, they also don't like to take days off unless it's for a paid trip home.

Contract employees work out of union halls or they work for a specific contractor. When they arrive on site for a project, such as a smelter shutdown, they are often ill prepared for the type of work they will be assigned.

Many contractors are usually involved in new installations of plant or equipment. Harsh environmental conditions prevalent in areas around the smelter do not sit well with them. Many show up for their first shift sporting beards that must be shaved. Supply and fit-testing of respirators, along with basic orientation, is required and time consuming because they have never worn a respirator before, let alone for 12 hours a shift.

The supply of new coveralls and other personal protective equipment is another sore point with regular employees. Their lament: "Bad enough they take our work and overtime, do we have to outfit them as well?" The supply of tools and equipment to contractors adds insult to injury.

An irony associated with contractors is site clean up after a job is complete. Sure, they will clean up their mess at the end of the job, but the problem is, you will pay for it dearly.

Don't get me wrong, contractors are unique, and they are necessary. No company can bankroll a workforce to take care of all its needs. The biggest problem is that they stick out in a small community to the point that it gets personal with some people. Having more privileges than the rest of the workforce, they are seen as "spoiled."

A typical example is that they are allowed to bring their personal vehicles on site in a great many cases while regular employees walk to their change house.

Contractors can make money, lots of money, and that, too, breeds jealousy.

When contractors work from approved engineering drawings they are not concerned if the drawings contain errors. They are not charged with the responsibility of correcting engineering mistakes as they go along. They follow the plan to the letter, even though they might well know it will have to be reworked. And guess who will make money on the rework?

When a company successfully bids on a contract, in some cases it goes to the union halls for their pool of labour. The union maintains a list of qualified trades and ensures that the work is being distributed fairly amongst its members. This means the contracting company can't pick and choose whom they will hire, except for the one-in-six rule!

The one-in-six rule allows the contracting company to pick anywhere on the union list for every sixth worker it requires. If a a worker chooses not to accept the work, his name will drop down the union list until it works its way towards the top again.

During the 1997 smelter shutdown, a major modification was made to both reverb furnace boilers. The contract company involved required a lot of specialized welder/boilermakers. Unfortunately, during the same time, a major project was taking place out west. As a result, the major contractor was only able to hire a very small number of employees with whom they had previously had experience. The rest were an unknown commodity. The result was not good – contractor workers not happy with the adverse conditions they were in!

Supervisors are key people who know must understand everyone within their charge, their strengths, weaknesses, training received, and needs. How can they be expected to take on that responsibility with any degree of success when they have only just been introduced to those individuals?

The supervisor is held accountable under the Workplace Safety and Health Act not to assign work that is outside the employee's capabilities. This is much less of an issue with regular company employees who can work for the same supervisor for many years.

Contractors are used to fill the void in manpower when special projects are created, or major shutdowns occur. The distain for contractors stems from a fear that contracting out will diminish the regular workforce and weaken the unions by having fewer members in their ranks. Ironically, many contractors work out of union halls.

Another reason they are not embraced by the general populous of the community, particularly if they live away from the area and are staying "in camp," is that money earned in the community doesn't get spent there.

The general workforce keeps a wary eye on contractors, keeping them under close scrutiny, particularly when it comes to safety or rule violations. Any discrepancies are quickly pointed out, yet many of the same people would never consider mentioning to a fellow worker that they should be wearing their safety glasses, yet they would rat out a contractor any time.

Most contractors are highly skilled and hard working. In preference to sitting in camp twiddling their thumbs, they prefer to work long hours, usually at least 12, and for long periods before days off, which are called RAP days ("rest and pussy," for the unenlightened).

However, because the good, the bad, and the ugly exist in all work groups, several specific incidents involving contractors are worth mentioning.

One time, a maintenance building was having an extension put on to accommodate a new surface garage and carpenters' shop. Various contractors were involved in the project and one group was using scaffolding in the work.

Tragically, an employee who was working for the City of Flin Flon at the time, fell from scaffolding he was using in the city's garage and died from his injuries. The workplace government inspectors issued a preliminary report within days to warn other scaffold users of their initial findings, which was very unusual because investigations of that nature usually take time. It is not unusual for months to go by before any recommendations are put forward.

The Workplace Safety Division released information that indicated the employee had fallen from the top deck of rolling scaffolding that was being moved at the time. The reason they had chosen to issue this finding so early was to warn other scaffold users of the potential consequences of moving scaffolding that was occupied.

When we received this information in the form of a bulletin from the workplace division, we immediately shared it with all crews using scaffolding on a regular basis. Knowing the contractor crew working on the building extension was using scaffolding, we brought in that crew and their supervisor to be briefed on the city worker incident and findings.

The next day, on a routine visit to the building extension to check on work in progress, I encountered two contractor workers who had decided to have a race to the top of a four-lift, partly erected scaffold while being egged on by their supervisor.

I witnessed a lot over nearly 50 years in the workplace, but I cannot recall anything close to this, nor could I even believe such of thing could happen given what had just taken place. That situation was a bit of the ugly.

In another contractor-related incident, while on a plant tour with the company's fire chief and plant protection officer, we got a radio call from the plant protection officer at the main gate. Assistance was being requested.

We arrived at the scene to find the traffic barrier down and an empty three-quarter ton crew cab truck parked up against it. Six contractors, including their supervisor, were waiting for us in the guard shack with the PPO.

The PPO stated that the crew cab, along with its occupants, had pulled up at the barrier to exit the site. As he was just about to raise the barrier, he noticed one of the passengers appeared to be holding a beer bottle in his hand. He left the barrier down and called us for assistance, then asked the contractors to wait until we arrived.

The chief asked the men assembled for an explanation. One of the contractors stated that an empty beer bottle was rolling around on the floor of the vehicle, so he had picked it up. The PPO at the gate must have seen it in his hand, he said, adding that it was an old empty bottle and that he had not been drinking.

The chief and I then went out to the vehicle. On the front seat was the empty beer bottle in question. We checked the rest of the vehicle and no other bottles were found in the cab. In the back of the truck's open box along with some other debris was a 12-pack of empty bottles with one missing. The chief took the empty bottle that was found in the cab and turned it upside down. Not one drop came out of it.

Back in the guard shack, the crew was told that beer bottles, empty or otherwise, must not be brought on site and to clean out the back of the crew cab and ensure that it remained that way. Because the beer bottle in question had appeared dry, the chief was prepared to give them the benefit of a doubt and no further action would be taken. They could all leave.

As the chief and I turned away from the group to continue our tour. A voice from the group, their supervisor, said, "Gee, I hope you're not going to tell Mommy."

Talk about not knowing when you're ahead, or when to keep your mouth shut! It was unbelievable, particularly because it came from the supervisor. What a shining beacon of light and wisdom! What an example to set as a leader!

A matter that so easily could have ended amicably was brought back to life like a Phoenix from the ashes with a couple of misspoken words.

Another incident involving contractors that could easily have been a fatality ended in a faint scratch on the back of an employee's hand. The scratch was caused when a piece of steel weighing around five pounds fell over 30 feet, grazing him on the way down.

Several key lessons came from the resulting investigation. Even though the outcome was minor, it was recognized that things could have been a lot worse. Always factor in potential consequences when determining how in-depth an investigation should be.

It was determined that the contractor had been hired to remove an old conveyor system that was no longer used. It was just below the rafters of a large concentrate-handling building used to store and blend concentrate ore. Half a dozen contractor workers were involved.

A safe-work plan used to identify all potential hazards that might exist throughout the scope of work had been drawn up prior to the start of the job. Once hazards have been identified, control measures are put in place to mitigate them to an acceptable level.

Sounds a little complicated but it's not. It's just a checklist of items to consider, which might include such things as whether the task involves working at heights; does it pose a risk of falling objects; does it include burning, cutting or welding; does the task expose workers to dust?

Once everything has been identified and agreed to, the list of hazards forms the basis for determining which controls are to be used. Working at heights may mean the use of fall protection or guard railing. Exposure to dust may require the use of respirators, dust goggles, barrier cream, or gloves.

Once complete, the safe-work plan is given a final review by workers and contractor supervisors to ensure that they are aware of all hazards associated with their work, and that they have been addressed. The safe-work plan is then signed off by all parties and forms the basis for how the work is to be done.

When the completed safe-work plan for this particular job was reviewed as part of the investigation, it was noted that the risk of falling objects had been correctly identified and that the control measure was to have the area below the work in progress restricted with the use of red barrier tape and Keep-Out warnings.

An information tag was to be placed on the barrier tape at intervals along its length, giving details of date, time and reason for placement in accordance with the company's barrier-tape policy. The only way anyone could gain access to the restricted area beyond the tape was by permission from the person who put up the tape.

So how does anyone manage to get hit by a falling object inside a restricted area? Two scenarios come to mind. Either the employee who got hit crossed under the barrier tape and was unauthorized to enter the restricted area, or the barrier tape had not been properly put in place as required by the safe-work plan.

In defence of his company, the contract supervisor offered the following explanation.

"Do you realize that had we complied with the safe-work plan and placed the barrier tape in position, we would have effectively shut down your operation because the trucks bringing concentrate into the building would not have been able to enter it?"

Wow! We had a contractor who believed he could control the company's operation! Why had he not voiced that concern during development of the safe-work plan? After all, barrier tape to restrict an area is only one of a host of controls that might have been considered had he spoken up. A flagman could have been used to restrict the area. The work above could have been shut down when trucks needed to enter the building. The work could have been performed on the night shift when trucks did not need to enter the area. The list goes on.

The contractor had missed the whole purpose of having a safe-work plan. It isn't just a piece of paper! It's an agreement by all concerned on what is required to do the job without somebody getting hurt. In this case, had the falling steel hit the employee anywhere else on his body, other than barely on the back of his hand, he could easily have been killed.

When it comes to safety, contracting companies have come a long way over the past 30 years. Their performance is being measured and their injuries scrutinized. Programs and initiatives such as the Certificate of Recognition program provide acknowledgement and demonstrate levels of competency to companies that might consider hiring them. Some government tenders are not allowed to be bid on unless the contractor is CORE certified.

Having WCB payments up to date and other safety and health programs available is another way of ensuring that the contractor you are dealing with is above board.

Reputation also plays a key role in contractors getting tenders accepted. Nobody wants to hire someone or work for someone with an unacceptable injury frequency rate. It's not the lowest bid that necessarily gets the work; it's the one that can complete the work on time, within cost, and without anyone getting hurt.

Many years ago, a contractor hired at the mine met just one of these requirements, the lowest bid. His company was hired to demolish a building and his reputation was almost legendary. He was quite the character.

His vehicles and any equipment he had were old, poorly maintained, and somewhat reflected the rest of his business. Many of his crew were picked up as they walked out prison gates on the day they were released. He would park outside the prison waiting to recruit his next employee.

On the demolition contract, he, along with his four employees, had been employed for several months at the mine. During that time, he housed the crew in one of the apartment buildings in town. He bought them groceries as well as fishing licences and took them fishing on at least one occasion. All related expenses he incurred were itemized and deducted from his workers' pay cheques.

Every day that he and his crew were on site was a challenge. He was constantly having to be reminded of company safety expectations. When we found out that one of his employees had received a hand injury after trapping it in a pinch point, I went to the demolition site to see how he was doing and find out what had happened.

When I asked to speak to the injured employee, the company owner said that he no longer worked for them. I said that I hoped it was not because of the injury and he replied that, no, it was not. The reason he had been fired was because when he was injured, he was allowed to go back to the apartment earlier than the rest of the crew.

As expected, the injured employee went home and cooked supper for himself, eating two pork chops, one more than his ration. That meant that the one of the other crew members would not have anything for supper that evening.

"That was why I got rid of him," said his boss, adding that it had nothing to do with him getting hurt.

Contract companies like that one find it hard to survive in today's environment. Thank goodness!

.

The Supervision

It is a unique group of individuals who take on the mantel of supervision. Supervisors walk the line between being the company's agents or representatives and the workers. As coaches, mentors, team leaders, disciplinarians, and sometimes as friends, or enemies, they are where the action is and can have the most influence on the workplace and its people. They are certainly where it's at when things go wrong, the ones on the hot seat or firing line, and they get it from both sides.

Supervisors have few rights, are not protected by contract or union representatives, and struggle for their very existence. Many would willingly give up the torch for the security of less stressful positions.

Often, they have received little training in the art of supervision. Many are trapped and unhappy, and when they have reached the limits of their endurance, they easily break ranks at the expense of other supervisors or mangers. They have tried to test the waters of strict discipline, or have seen others do so, only to fail.

It is not like these people are a bad bunch. They truly are not, but they are trapped in a web and do not get the respect or recognition they deserve. The resources of the Human Resources Department, although available to supervisors, are seldom drawn upon because HR is seen by many as out of touch with the real world.

They struggle to successfully manage a group of employees fairly, keep them safe, efficient, and producing quality work with limited resources. How to do that consistently can truly be a good cop, bad cop scenario. How do you be all things to all people, and still be within budget... less 10 percent?

Some supervisors, unfortunately, do not get it! They fail because they miss one of the very basic principles of what a supervisor can and should be more than anything else – a leader!

One fundamental fact is that a supervisor's work group can be a mirror image of himself. They underestimate the influence they can have on their employees as their crews constantly scrutinize them. But it's not the big things that they are measured against.

Crews realize that most of the big stuff is outside their supervisors' control. What really counts are those little signals that are sent out every day... the tone in their voice when they are reading out a safety contact or bulletin, for example, or their facial expressions, or their interaction with line supervision.

A supervisor's loyalty is divided between his crew, the department, and the employer. Of all the qualities they need to have, the ability to be consistent and fair is uppermost. If this most important tool is missing from their toolbox, they can neither hire nor fire.

Many good supervisors are poached from the union ranks because the unions do a very good job of training their officials and executive membership. They get excellent training as shop stewards and union officers in such areas as contract and grievance procedures.

The only problem with this method of recruitment is the baggage they leave and the baggage that they bring with them. An ex-brother in a supervisory role is a target. The higher the position they left as a member of their union, the more unforgiving the general membership can be.

The higher they climb up the corporate ladder, the more they are resented by the rank and file, which is a factor that comes into play when disaster unfolds.

Who Do You Know?

It has been my experience that one of the significant influences on corporate culture, which existed in both companies I worked for, is the impact an external organization can have on management structure.

There is always the possibility of one candidate for a position having an edge over another when the interviewer has personal knowledge or is an acquaintance of one of the candidates. Since the beginning of time, nepotism has always been at play when positions are filled by personnel who might not have been awarded the job had the playing field been a level one.

There is a significant effect on morale and safety when a person is parachuted into a position not deserved, or when he turns out to be incompetent or unqualified.

When I was employed at the steelworks, one of the staff maintenance foremen was retiring after many years of service. His charge hand, who had dutifully served his boss for almost the same period, and had covered the position during vacations and illnesses, was a shew-in to take over. But the position was given to a person who had no idea about the area, the men, or the equipment for which he was responsible.

The one credential that the charge hand did not have over his new boss was that he was not a member of the Free Masons while the person who got the job, as well as the one who did the interviews, was.

I remember very well the disbelief by the rank and file within the area when the appointment was made. When the charge hand asked why he had been passed over for the position he was asked: "Why have you waited nearly 20 years to put in for a staff position? Where have you been till now?"

The charge hand also had to spend his remaining work years trying to teach the new kid on the block how things worked. It was not an easy task. After his new supervisor had been in the position for a number of weeks, he turned to his righthand man, the charge hand that had been overlooked, and asked which end of the high-speed tension line they were standing by, the start of it or the exit.

Now, I'm not suggesting for one moment that all Free Masons are bad people. I have met many throughout my career, and my own father became a Mason after he retired. There are good and bad in all walks of life. I can only relate the personal observation and experiences I have had over the years in the two large industries in which I have worked.

It would be fair to say there was a disproportionate number of Free Masons holding key maintenance, supervisory, and management positions when I joined Hudson Bay Mining and Smelting 37 years ago. That fact contributed to the culture that existed at that time. Some were qualified and competent to have filled their positions with or without being members of a lodge, but there were others who were in over their heads, to put it mildly.

The Masonic Lodge was, and still is, strategically placed a short walk from the main entrance of the company and what would have been the company apartments and company cottages. But today the company apartments and houses have been bulldozed and the Masonic Hall struggles to remain open.

That doesn't mean nepotism is dead; it still exists in other forms. The old boys club, senior mine and operations personnel, seem to flow fluently from one mining company to another, gaining ever more experience as they go. It's like a giant recycling program. One even managed to get recycled twice, much to the amazement of the rest of the workforce.

Out with the old and in with the new. The new bring innovative ideas they learn from previous employment, some of which are predestined to fail because the rank and file have seen it all before.

The new tend to time-out in less than five years. They either get booted out with the golden handshake or get promoted to a higher position with another mining company. This phenomenon has both a positive and a negative effect on the general workforce, which celebrates the demise of a manager or superintendent for whom they had no respect only to find out the incoming replacement is worse. Sometimes it's better the devil you know than the one you don't.

The Free Masons are just one of the many organizations that give support to local community projects and, given the population of Flin Flon and surrounding area, this speaks highly of the people who generously volunteer their time. You can join just about any group, but I don't think any have had more influence within the workforce than the Masons. Their reach is not confined to mining and steelmaking but crosses continents and all types of industries.

A very good friend of mine who worked in a paper mill received a staff assessment of 105 percent in December of 1997 yet was laid off on Jan. 18, 1998. He was a fully certified industrial mechanic, responsible for looking after 560 pieces of rotating equipment, some of it 25,000 HP motors driving refiners. The person who filled his position had no trade, no qualifications, zip – other than the fact he was a Mason.

Not only was my friend laid off at that time, but other supervisors also had the experience of being laid off and having Masons take over their positions. One such replacement could not even look up parts on a computer.

Another called my friend at home a few months after and asked him for advice. Apparently, one of his crew members had called him a F...ing arsehole and a moron in front of the whole crew. My friend's advice was to give the person a written warning and make sure other people knew it. The new guy did not heed the advice given because he did not like "personal confrontation," yet he was supposed to be a supervisor.

There are many negative aspects involved in a person filling a position for which he or she is either not qualified for or does not deserve to have in the first place. The effect on morale within the rest of the workforce can range from anger to disbelief. The values of good corporate governance are also undermined, which is hard to reverse once you have people in the management system who have no credibility with the general workforce.

And it's not just the Masons. I am only relating my personal experience. One employee once said to me, "Just wait until a Lions Club member, or an Elks member gets the boss's job, then these guys can look out."

I attended a conference a few years ago where one of the guest speakers, who was an HR specialist, spoke about the importance of hiring. He noted that most companies don't take into account that, "The next person that you put on your payroll has the potential to make or break your company."

I have not seen anyone break a company I have worked for, but I have seen some of the consequences that have occurred after some individuals have made decisions that cost thousands and, in some cases, even millions of dollars.

In 1968, Laurence J. Peter, a prominent Canadian scholar of education, conducted research that lead to the formulation of the *The Peter Principle*. He concluded in his book of the same name that within large corporations, people can get promoted beyond their competency level. The qualities and skills that made them stand out at one level might get them promoted into something they could be terrible at.

For example, a great mechanic does not necessarily make a good supervisor of mechanics. Likewise, a good teacher could be a lousy principal. A likely solution to this problem is to ensure adequate screening and training for employees receiving promotion.

Dr. Peter also argued that employees tend to remain in positions for which they are incompetent because it rarely is enough to cause them to be fired. Ordinarily, he noted, only extreme incompetence causes dismissal.

He summed up the Peter Principal with a twist to the adage, "Cream always rises to the top" by adding "until it sours."

A supervisor once questioned why he had to undergo accident investigation training. After all is said and done, he argued, the safety department had personnel who had more experience and training. They should be the ones to carry out investigations, which would allow him more time to do what he was supposed to do, supervise!

My response to his rationale was that I wouldn't want to work for him. I wouldn't want to work for anyone who didn't want to know and fully understand what, why, and how one of his subordinates got injured, and who felt that it was someone else's job to find out.

Respect is one of the most important attributes of any good person, but especially of a leader of men and women. In order to gain respect, you must give it. You can try to be respectful, but at the end of the day, gaining respect must be earned. Once you have the respect of others, it must be maintained and nurtured constantly because it can easily be lost. And once you lose respect, it's almost impossible to get it back.

A janitor had to clean a two-storey office building every night. With no elevator in the building and a fairly steep flight of stairs between floors, she asked her supervisor if an additional vacuum cleaner could be purchased. A vacuum could then be stored and used on each floor. That would eliminate the need to carry one up and down the stairs every night and thereby prevent the possibility of a back injury. Plus, the cost of another machine was minimal but the person with the authority to purchase an additional vacuum cleaner brushed aside the request with, "No darn way!"

What a missed opportunity to let a worker know that she was valued more than a simple item like an additional vacuum cleaner.

A very good friend of mine owned a small successful business installing television satellite receivers on the roofs of homes. He and his son who worked for him used a unique ladder system to gain access to the rooftops. The ladder was attached to a customer's home by means of a metal brace bolted to the side of the house and attached to an appropriate rung of the ladder. This method guaranteed access to the ladder, which could not move while somebody was using it.

A single hole had to be drilled into the brickwork of the home to accommodate the brace. Once the roof work was completed, the bolt was removed and a suitably coloured plastic filler was injected into the hole, leaving its location almost impossible to detect. My friend had installed hundreds of receivers in this manner without incident.

One day he received a call from a new customer requesting an installation. When told that a hole was going to be drilled to accommodate the ladder safety brace, the homeowner replied, "No darn way."

My friend replied, "I will not put my life, or that of my son on the line for the sake of your not having a hole in your brickwork. You are going to have to find another company to do your installation. Goodbye!"

While on their monthly tours, safety committees do a great job of identifying unsafe conditions. The challenge for any supervisor is to get ahead of the game and not allow a walk-through of his/her area of responsibility to come up with a list of items that need to be addressed.

It doesn't necessarily have to be a committee, it could be an auditor, government official, workplace health and safety inspector, or their boss who spots something unsafe. Does this mean the supervisor is blind, uncaring, or just too busy to take care of the fundamentals of making sure his area is free of hazards and meets all regulatory requirements. No! It's a lack of recognition by supervisors of the amount of control and influence they have over the resources that they manage.

Housekeeping is a prime example. An area under the responsibility of a supervisor, whether it's neat and tidy or a total disaster, directly reflects that supervisor and his crew. The supervisor can assign subordinates to clean-up duties and keep doing so until he is satisfied with the results. He can even make cleanup a part of every work assignment, but some seldom do.

The auditing process has three methods of verification: personal observation, employee interviews, and documentation/record verification. Each method has its flaws but a combination of two out of three, or use of all three methods, gives a greater level of confidence in the auditor's findings on any single conformance or non-conformance.

Each method of auditing can provide misleading information and should never be used on its own merit in establishing facts.

For instance, several employees at a workplace complained that they were not receiving their weekly half-hour safety contact with their direct supervisor.

The policy at the company was for the frontline supervisors to meet with their crews at least once a week and have a general discussion on a safety item, in order to get feedback on any safety issues the crew might have. Theme topics, such as use of scaling bars, wheel chock requirements, etc., were sometimes used to get the conversation started. Who attended the meetings and the topics covered were recorded. Half an hour was allowed for such meetings.

Records of crew meetings in the work area were checked for the previous six-month period, revealing that the crew in question had documented evidence that they had received a safety contact every week during that six-month period. The topic of the contact was listed, along with a list of attendees.

The next part of the audit was spent talking individually to members of the crew and asking them if they could remember the topic of last week's safety contact. The response was unanimous. They all said they had not received a safety contact for months.

The crew's supervisor was then asked for an explanation of the conflicting evidence. He agreed with the findings from the personal interviews. He had used the index from the back of the Safety Contact Book of suggested topics and his crew list to falsify the records to show that contacts had taken place when they had not.

Another example that came to light was during an audit of completed confined-space permits, which had been handed in by supervisors over the preceding 12 months. One of the questions supervisors were required to answer on the permit was: "Does the confined-space attendant have current first aid training? Yes or No?

The audit findings revealed that by far the majority of permits failed to identify that this question had even been addressed. The Yes or No option had just been left blank.

The saying, "Never ask a question that you don't want to hear the answer to," was particularly true in this case because "No" would have meant the prospective candidate for the role of confined-space attendant had just disqualified himself.

A new search to fill the position would have to begin, which might mean going beyond the personnel in the immediate area, or on that shift, to find someone with the necessary qualifications. Again, this would be time consuming, the work could not be started, and it could involve calling somebody out on overtime.

Despite the fact that the Workplace Safety and Health Regulations require personnel to have current first aid training in order to be a confined-space attendant, some supervisors had chosen to roll the dice in the hope that the attendant would never be confronted with a situation during work that would require him to use first aid.

In the third example of audit findings in relation to record checks and verification, a supervisor was handed a risk assessment of the checks that had been made prior to an electrical worker's working near energized equipment. The assessment also included what steps would be taken if something were to go wrong that would create an emergency, such as if electrical contact was made or an arc flash situation occurred. The requirement was that the person doing the job would complete the assessment detailing personal protective equipment requirements and potential severity of exposure.

The assessment would then be handed in to the supervisor, who was required to review and file it for a year. A random review by the auditor of the previous six months of completed risk assessments provided via the supervisor's files, revealed one that raised both the supervisor and the auditor's eyebrows. In filling out the risk assessment, the electrical worker had written, "Who the Fuck cares?" in the space provided for details of the rescue plan.

The irony was that the response to the question took several months to answer, essentially re-enforcing the individual's comment, and would never have happened if the risk assessment had not been randomly selected in the audit process. It would seem that, indeed, nobody did care.

The individual who wrote the comment was told, "Yes, we do care. We care deeply that when you work around energized equipment, you have taken the time to consider what you need and how you are going to complete the work safely.

The point is that all supervisors, old and new, sometimes overwhelmed by endless paperwork, make poor choices. Don't falsify records! Don't assign work unless you are sure the person is qualified to do it, and don't sign and file anything you haven't read.

Safety and Health Committees

An agreement struck by the federal government and the Manitoba and Saskatchewan governments in the early 80s gave some credibility to a process that previously had each of these players having a finger in the safety and health pie. This was, in part, because HBMS straddled both provinces and because the War Measures Act of the 1940s had not been rescinded.

Prior to the Province of Manitoba Workplace Safety and Health legislation being adopted as the legal standard to work to, confusion existed when mines inspectors from all three governments rolled into town, mostly on separate days and with different missions.

Two levels of safety and health committees existed within the company, and I was very fortunate over the course of my career to have had the support of many dedicated health and safety co-workers and union health and safety committee members and representatives.

The department safety committees, made up of representatives from unions and management, are structured to the terms of the Manitoba Workplace Safety and Health Act. They meet and complete workplace inspections each month.

Safety concerns are documented through meeting minutes that are posted in work areas and sent to the Mines Branch. Committees have a certain amount of leverage and credibility so, depending on the area, they can be very effective at improving workplace conditions.

Supervisors sometimes feed issues to the Safety and Health Committee that they have failed to address themselves due to budget restraints. The number of committees varies but the core committees are headed jointly by management and union appointees.

Three core groups investigated the disaster at the smelter in 2000: The Mines Inspection Branch, the RCMP, and the Smelter Safety and Health Committee.

A Mines Branch investigation is done in conjunction with the RCMP. Mines inspectors look to see that all provincial regulations were adhered to leading up to an accident and to recommend changes to legislation if deficiencies are found. Charges under the Workplace Safety and Health Act may also be laid as a result of an investigation.

As a rule, an RCMP investigation centres on the need to establish if criminal charges are warranted against individuals as a result of negligence or willful intent.

Generally, the Safety and Health Committee forwards the results of its investigations to the Mines Branch to support the findings of the branch and to identify anything that may have been overlooked. Interviews are held independently, and the process can be long and painstaking.

Collation between statements and witnesses must be consistent and cross referenced to ensure accuracy.

Bias, perceptions, and hearsay must be weeded out. The Mines Branch, in conjunction with the RCMP, takes statements sworn under oath, which carry the weight of law. Statements obtained by the safety committee are voluntary submissions and are not subjected to the same scrutiny.

Employees who fail to co-operate with the Safety and Health Branch can be charged under the Workplace Safety and Health Act, although this has seldom if ever been put to the test.

The second level of the safety committee (Tier 2) was formed as part of the collective bargaining agreement but its purpose was difficult to establish. It was made up of senior management from a cross section of the operation, and an equal number of union-appointed safety representatives. It was, at one time, seen as a vehicle to resolve items that appeared on the departmental safety minutes for an unacceptable time. With no budget or defined mandate to resolve issues, it failed in many respects.

More recently, the Tier 2 committee tried to address the issue of plant policy and procedures but again did not meet the expectations of its members or of the general workforce. In order for a procedure to be successful, it has to be developed by the employees who are expected to work to it. Tier 2 became a rubber stamp that only slowed the process down.

In terms of policy development, it is the prerogative of management to issue policy. Unions would be in a very uncomfortable position fulfilling the role of policy makers, but union co-chairs took the initiative to hold monthly meetings to discuss common issues of concern.

Full-time safety personnel included a superintendent of loss control, WCB claims administrator, modified work supervisor, six department loss-control co-ordinators, and a full-time safety representative nominated by the largest union (The Steelworkers).

Expectations ran high going into the shutdown. The company had celebrated back to back years of best safety performance measured by lost-time accidents. There seemed to be a general feeling that the smelter shutdown of 2000 could be achieved without a lost-time accident. Talk of safety incentives and how to recognize such a performance consumed sub-committee meetings leading up to the shutdown.

New methods and equipment were going to be used to reduce the heavy physical labour that was traditional with shutdowns that had gone before. A D7 Cat was to replace the skidder for furnace brick removal and remote controlled Brokk machines would replace men on jackhammers.

II

WORK SHOULDN'T HURT

E very year an unacceptable number of workplaces lose their most valuable assets, their workers, to life-changing injuries and death.

Having spent the best part of 50 years in steelmaking and mining, the last 28 in risk management or, dare I say, health and safety, I thought it might be of some benefit to share some of my experiences and insight in an attempt to help employees, employers, supervisors and workers, owners and shareholders in understanding what it takes to provide safe work.

Examples used are not to cast blame or point fingers at accident victims. They are used as learning opportunities in the hope that by increasing awareness about why and how accidents occur, we can benefit from those experiences, which is the only benefit to be derived from accidents. Lessons must be learned and shared, or they will be repeated.

The accidents discussed in this book in no way suggest apathy on the part of any company, particularly the two for which I have had the pleasure of working. What has happened in the past is not a reflection of their commitment or lack of commitment to providing a safe place for people to work.

In fact, many larger corporations are charged with the additional responsibility and subject to greater scrutiny than smaller companies. Many of the larger mining, steelmaking, and chemical industries are at the forefront in helping set the standards and regulations that others then rely on.

In Search of Zero

The holy grail of most corporations is to maximize profits while enjoying an accident-free workplace. One of the major challenges in pursuing this holy grail is that whenever people are employed to perform work they are invariably put at some sort of risk. If followed to the letter, the adage, "Nobody moves, nobody gets hurt," would achieve an accident-free workplace, but it wouldn't be a very productive or practical approach.

A common practice in large organizations is to set goals at the beginning of each year in order to reduce accident incidents. Yet it would not be well received for companies to announce their objective for the coming year is to have just five serious injures instead of the 10 they had the previous year. A 50 percent reduction is a lofty goal, but no planned number of accidents would seem to be appropriate.

However, the best approach is to focus on reducing the likelihood of any accidents by eliminating some of the many contributing factors that caused them in the first place. If you believe all accidents can be eliminated, that's good, but is it realistic or just a pipe dream?

A safe workplace must be an expectation for everyone, yet that is like trying to forecast when and where the next earthquake will occur. Just when you think you have everything under control, you are reminded of how fragile we humans can be.

One of the outcomes from the aftermath of the smelter explosion that occurred Aug. 8, 2000, was the overwhelming desire to ensure nothing like that could ever happen again. Indeed, the year 2000 proved to be a disastrous year in terms of health and safety for Anglo American, Hudson Bay Mining's parent company at the time. All told, Anglo had over 70 fatalities throughout their worldwide operations in that single year. Something had to be done, and quickly.

Anglo commissioned a retired, soft-spoken DuPont executive, Professor Peter Mckie, to do a study on the fatalities to determine what had caused so many people to lose their lives on the job.

After an extensive review, he concluded that only a relatively small number of tasks were being performed when the fatalities occurred. In fact, seven tasks had accounted for all the fatalities. He also determined that those tasks were performed to different standards, rules, or regulations depending on their geographical location.

Working at heights was one of those seven tasks identified in the review. Manitoba Workplace Safety and Health regulations called for training, specialized PPE to be worn, guard rails, physical barriers, etc. as ways to prevent falls. I am reasonably certain that anyone who has visited a developing country has seen work being performed at heights that did not incorporate any of these controls.

Standards, therefore, had to be established at all Anglo work sites, which, as a minimum, had to meet regulatory requirements for that location. If regulations did not exist, or were considered inadequate, then Anglo's own standards would be used, based on best practices, or those being used at other sites where strong regulatory requirements were in place.

The Golden Rules were introduced as a result for all high-risk activities throughout Anglo's worksites. They included confined-space entry, working at heights, vehicle safety, working in hot metal areas, working around energized equipment, excavation work, use of cranes and lifting equipment, and underground mining operations.

Health and safety have received a bad rap over the last couple of decades. Regulators have redefined the landscape of the workplace in very descriptive terms of reference, which have been imposed on both the employer and employees. In some cases, this was driven from the need to combat the never-ending spiral of serious workplace injuries and fatalities, which is a good thing because the definition of insanity is to continue doing the same thing while expecting different results.

We need to change! We need to learn from the lessons that people have suffered through, and for which they have paid a high price.

The workplace is constantly evolving, and we must learn to evolve with it. What once was common practice is now deplorable. For example, one of the work areas I was assigned to in the steelworks in the late 60s and early 70s was the cold mill. It consisted of three noisy temper mills, high-speed cut up lines, and re-shears.

When I returned for a visit many years later, nobody was allowed into the building without wearing hearing protection. Nothing inside the building to do with noise levels had changed, only the awareness that hearing impairment was almost rampant among cold mill workers and that something had to be done.

Another example from the same era is exposure to second-hand cigarette smoke. Lunch areas, meeting rooms, even airplanes, restaurants, bars, etc. were once filled with the blue haze of tobacco smoke. Not anymore! Regulations have come into effect to combat the ill health caused by long-term exposure to tobacco smoke.

One of the biggest challenges is the basic understanding that most safety issues are common sense. A good example is the fact that if an object is traveling in a container that is unrestrained at 80 km/h and then comes to an instant stop, the contents of that container are going to keep traveling – basic law of physics! It does not take a rocket scientist to determine that seatbelts were designed to combat personal injury and save lives.

You would think that anyone who gets into a vehicle would automatically secure themselves. If that were the case our hospitals and cemeteries would have fewer occupants. And our police officers and courtrooms would far less busy.

Understanding why people choose to roll the dice and double down when it comes to risk taking is one of the most interesting facets of health and safety today and, again, one of its biggest hurdles to be addressed.

Workplace Inspections

Beauty is in the eye of the beholder. Cleanliness is next to Godliness. Good housekeeping is a place for everything and everything in its place. We have all heard these and similar little bits of wisdom.

Housekeeping or, rather, good housekeeping, plays an important role in accident prevention. Poor housekeeping reflects other things, such as low morale, improper supervision, ineffective work practices, etc.

In all my years of experience, I never once heard a supervisor ask one of his subordinates to put the broom away and stop cleaning up. Yet, when an area is in disarray, it is a direct reflection of how much a supervisor values order in the workplace, and what kind of priority he or she gives it. It is the supervisor who sets the tone and assigns work.

When I first began working at a mine in a surface machine shop, the last two hours on a Friday afternoon were dedicated to cleaning up. It was probably seen as the least productive time in terms of getting anything significant done. It was too late to start anything major, and everyone was looking forward to the weekend off. But it was a good clean up with everyone pulling together and, just before quitting time, the place was transformed into what it should be. The shop would remain empty and looking pristine for the weekend before the onslaught of another week.

The problem with this type of cleaning cycle was that at any given time between Monday to that couple of hours late on Friday afternoon, the place could be a bit of a mess, or worse! Certainly, time was allotted toward the end of each day for some general tidying up, usually about 15 minutes or so, but for some reason, nothing seemed to work in some of areas.

If I was to point out one area that did get it right in the later years it would be the welding/boilermaker shop. You could walk through that area at any time of the day or week and the place always looked great. In fact, I would often tell people that if they ever wanted to see what good housekeeping looks like, to go visit the boilermakers' section of the machine shop, or the pipe shop in the Flin Flon mill.

The people who worked there and the people who supervised those two areas realized that an area is easier to maintain if housekeeping is practised all the time, not just at the end of the day or week.

When it comes to inspections, large organization certainly get their fair share of them. The safety committee tours through all the areas once a month and usually submits a list of items that need attention. The supervisor does a formal inspection once a beat underground, and once a week on the surface.

Plant protection people tour all the areas looking at items such as fire suppression systems and fire extinguishers. Internal and external auditors tour areas looking for compliance to standards.

Managers and superintendents tour through the areas quarterly and government officers, such as mines inspectors, carry out regular inspections looking for compliance to regulations.

One would think that with all those inspections being carried out by so many different groups of individuals, nothing would be found deficient. Yet, it would seldom be the case that a clean sheet would be generated on inspection reports.

One of the lessons I learned from an old pro when I entered the safety and health profession was to be careful not to overwhelm people responsible for an area you are inspecting. If you look hard and long enough and get into the corners, you will generally find something that needs attention.

If you get too picky or generate a list of deficiencies that would choke a horse, then the exercise becomes counterproductive. I'm not suggesting you should ignore the obvious or turn a blind eye. For example, a friend of mine owned three stores on the east coast. One was brand new. Prior to the official opening, he told me that a government inspector had visited his new store and spent an extraordinary amount of time walking the aisles and scrutinizing every square foot of the premises.

Finally, he told my friend everything was pretty good. However, he had to issue him an order to have a lock placed on the electrical lighting panel breaker box. The box was not dissimilar to the type you have at home.

Bear in mind, this government inspector was not an electrical inspector. The electrical work had already been inspected and had complied with all permits and electrical codes.

My friend questioned the validity of having to place a padlock on the offending breaker panel box. The inspector thought that it would be a good idea to prevent members of his staff gaining access to it.

"But they may need to gain access to reset a tripped breaker," my friend replied.

"Then place the key to the padlock on a hook next to the panel," said the inspector.

Situations like that give safety a bad name and cause people who hold positions of trust to lose credibility. It was as if the inspector needed to find something wrong to justify his visit. If he couldn't find something he could write down, it might seem as though he hadn't even been there.

I have done hundreds of workplace inspections in my time. I have toured with mines inspectors, safety committees, supervisors, managers, fire chiefs, internal and external auditors. It's sometimes okay not to find something and give a supervisor or crew a pat on the back and acknowledgement them for a job well done.

There is a saying in the auditing business. "In God we trust, everyone else we audit." As an internal auditor, and external one for that matter, you are looking for compliance to standards.

To ensure standards are followed, verification by an auditor takes place in three ways. The first is through record checks, paperwork, training records, meeting minutes, inspection reports, etc.

The second is by interview: asking the people who know or should know about the particular standard that is being audited, how it is applied, and their personal knowledge of its application.

The third verification takes place through physical tours of the workplace, where a standard or procedure or rule is observed to see if it is being followed. A non-conformance is any deviation from the standard.

Sounds simple, but each one of these verifications can have its flaws, such as inspection reports being falsified. A case in point: In a 24-hour period, meter recordings needed to be taken on two different shifts. Over a four-day period, the recordings were out of spec half the time. The times that they were recorded accurately was when they were out of spec. The time they were falsified was when they were recorded as being in spec – what they should have been not what they were!

During interviews, the auditor may get told what the person being interviewed thinks the interviewer needs to hear, not necessarily what is happening.

Finally, verification by observation can also be flawed. A story going around the plant one time involved a mines inspector on a routine tour underground, along with a supervisor and union health and safety representative. When they came around a corner into a drift, a mine employee some distance ahead of them appeared to have been smoking a cigarette. The inspector turned to the supervisor and asked him if he saw the employee smoking. The supervisor stated that he wasn't certain. The inspector then turned to the union safety representative who stated that he never saw a thing.

Most people, when they are observed and know the correct way of doing a job will do it correctly. Unfortunately, human nature being what it is, some people are apt to take shortcuts if they know they can get away with it. The challenge for any supervisor is to have your crew work the way they should, whether you are present or not.

One of the things I always thought was interesting was working with professional auditors. These people do nothing else but travel the country and, in some cases, the world, scrutinizing workplaces to various international standards. They are pros at what documents to look for and how to interview people. They also have a keen eye. They know just what questions to ask to get the information they need. I used to marvel at the way they framed questions. They are highly trained experts in production and environmental issues and have an exceptional understanding of the processes they are auditing.

They could randomly pick half a dozen documents from a stack of hundreds and find the ones they needed that could support their findings. They could observe things on tours that previous inspections had missed. But in the end, they, too, proved to be human. They did miss things. Even with all their experience, training and knowledge they were not infallible.

On one occasion during a review of an emergency procedures manual, the auditor asked what provision had been made in the event of a tsunami. The question would have been perfectly legitimate if we hadn't been pretty much in the centre of Canada's land mass.

On another occasion, their audit plan man hours were not adding up, so they needed to work in an extra shift. Not to fulfill their commitment of a certain number of auditing hours was not an option. Rather than backtrack to spend more time at the large flagship mine they had already visited they chose to take the easier way out and double down on the smaller mine they were currently at.

Auditors have human frailties as well. That mine had very little time left before it was scheduled to close permanently and had only a small number of employees to sample.

Audits are necessary, what gets measured is more likely to get done. When an organization is audited, it measures its strengths and weaknesses. If continual improvement is one of the corporate objectives, which it should be, then management needs to know where to channel resources and correct deficiencies.

Audit reports, as well as inspection reports, should always incorporate positive acknowledgements. To simply produce a list of nonconformances is not only discouraging, but also counterproductive. The "demeanour" of an auditor is important but being a "meaner" auditor is not.

Some tips for people being audited:
- Tell the truth; they can spot BS a mile away!
- Only answer the questions being asked.
- Don't volunteer information or documents that have not been asked for.
- Feed them well.

Training and Experience

Some of the first questions that get asked during an accident/incident investigation:
- What training have the personnel received?
- How long have they been performing the task?
- How much experience do they have?

One of the best pieces of advice I was given the day after I finished my four-year apprenticeship as a maintenance fitter (millwright) was to remember that the learning continues.

"Nobody waved a wand and gave you any more knowledge than you had yesterday," said one of my senior fellow craftsmen.

At 20 years of age, I had the world at my feet. As a qualified tradesman, I was assigned a "fitter's mate," who was 40 years my senior. His job was to carry my tools to the job, clean the job down prior to me working on it, hand me my tools as I needed them, clean them when I was done, and put them away in my locker to await my next assignment.

My mate's other duties included making me a great cup of tea. He was a wonderful man and he loved his job. He knew more about how to fix the wide variety of mechanical equipment we were confronted with than most tradesmen. His years of experience of passing wrenches and watching closely as his charge got things back up and running was invaluable to me.

I would try to wrestle my tool bag away from him, wanting to carry it myself and share the load but he would have none of that. I was very fortunate to have him as a mate, and as a friend.

I also drew on the experience of the lead operators on the high-speed lines and temper mills that we repaired. They, too, had been exposed to similar breakdowns in the past so the time saved in not having to fault-find as much as I would have without them was valuable, especially when production down time due breakdowns was measured in minutes and Pounds Stirling. Sure, I was no longer an apprentice, but it can take years to hone your craft, and you never stop learning.

Education vs. experience

One of the interesting conflicts I encountered later in my career had to do with the difference between experience and education. When metallurgists with degrees wanted to make adjustments to the process in copper and zinc recovery, they came up against less educated but more experienced process operators.

The two groups constantly battled each other with very little respect for their respective backgrounds. The process operator would have worked in every aspect of metal recovery from grinding the ore through the crushers, rod mills and ball mills to the floatation cells and, eventually, to concentrate. Their many years of experience gave them confidence in what adjustments in the circuit needed to be made to maximize recovery and prevent product going to waste.

In contrast, the young metallurgist who had spent years in university studying the fine art of metal production had the same goal as the process operator. Neither wanted to see the efforts of so many end up in the tailings pond. Yet seldom could they align.

When it comes to workplace training, it's a question of where you start. How much information are you going to provide to a new employee without being seen as simply going through the motions?

Of course, there are the legislative requirements to consider and they can be extensive, depending on the type of work and exposures the employee is going to encounter performing everyday duties. Just the basics include such things as workplace hazardous information systems, the right to know, and the right to refuse. They might require First Aid and CPR training. The list is endless, and that doesn't include company policies, procedures, rules, etc. And, of course, employees also require training in the work they are expected to do, but training takes away from the bottom line. It can be very expensive and, in some cases, is a waste of time and valuable resources.

When companies start to feel the pinch, training is one of the first targets when belts are tightened. Unfortunately, it's at the expense of programs that yield long-term benefits rather than short-term savings. When austerity measures need to be taken, apprenticeship programs traditionally are put on the chopping block early.

As well, when it comes to training, one size doesn't fit all. For instance, the requirement that forklift operators need to be certified to operate in Manitoba. Everyone agrees that makes sense, but when it comes to recertification, it starts to get fuzzy.

Some operators spend five to six hours a shift operating a forklift. After three years, they are, no doubt, more proficient in the operation of their equipment than any trainer. Trainers seldom, if ever, have that amount of time behind the controls unless, of course, your best operator becomes the trainer. The only problem with that scenario is that being a good operator does not necessarily make one a good trainer. Being able to operate a piece of equipment is one thing, but trainers also need to have good communication and training skills.

Over the years, I have seen a lot of money wasted on training through the shotgun approach, which happens when individuals are trained to allow the employer flexibility in work assignments. Another example of wasting training dollars is when someone is to be trained who doesn't need to be trained, just to get the training numbers up. I had someone who was one week away from retirement attending my aerial lift training class. Training someone for the sake of training on the off chance he might need it is not a good idea.

It's one thing to have a forklift and 10 guys on a crew certified to operate it, but if eight of the 10 only get to do so once or twice a year, they have probably not been able to hone their skills as much as the two regular operators. That is where the experience factor plays such an important role.

Applying what has been learned during training on a regular basis after training is the most valuable part of the whole process. Unfortunately, this doesn't happen as often as it should. In fact, some employees seldom, if ever, get to use some of the training they receive.

The more complex tasks generally have procedures associated with them. Again, a good procedure ensures that the person carrying out a task is doing it consistently. The downside to written work procedures is ensuring they are available to the person who needs to use them. They can tend to sit in filing cabinets or on computers only to see the light of day when the auditor comes along, or when an accident takes place.

Ensuring that your employees know the procedures they are expected to follow and have easy access to them when they may need them is paramount.

Another area to keep in mind when it comes to training is employee turnover. Companies that have high turnover rates keep pouring more and more money into providing training only to see it walk out the door. The hard question to be asked of companies facing this dilemma is why people don't want to stay with them.

A friend of mine who ran a business in a large city said something that I found intriguing. He was telling me that his company had high employee turnover. His reason for it was that he could only offer them a job, he could not offer them a career.

He paid a reasonable wage, much higher than the required minimum, but if similar work could be found in the neighbourhood for 25 cents an hour more, he knew many of his workers would take it. They were good workers and he, no doubt, was a good boss, but there was no sense of loyalty or commitment to make them want to stay. It was purely financial.

However, keeping employees happy at work sometimes isn't always about the money. If they don't feel valued or have a sense that they don't make a difference, they will want to move on. Over the years, I have seen many very good people leave for these reasons.

When I came to Flin Flon 39 years ago, Hudbay had invested heavily in the community. The company had put money into things that it hoped would help attract and keep people in the community, giving support to a golf course, swimming pool, community centre, hockey arena, beach concession, tennis courts, and a children's playground. The company was the hub of the community and its employees appreciated the facilities it provided.

Many of those facilities helped mothers with young children settle into the community. There is a lot of truth in the saying, "Happy wife, happy life."

Unfortunately, in time the company made the decision that it was in the mining business, not the entertainment business, and started to pull away from community projects it had once nurtured.

You can put a dollar figure on the amount of money they saved by their change in direction but what is more difficult to access is how much it influenced people deciding to seek greener pastures. It may not have changed employees who had come from larger communities who could not make the adjustment needed to survive in a much smaller place, but it may well have kept those who were used to small town life.

Training delivery methods vary, and all have their pros and cons. The trend in recent years has been to sit the student in front of a computer whenever practical. This method ensures the material is delivered constantly. A test is usually administered afterwards with a pass or fail grade. Typical lesson plans delivered using this method included the Workplace Hazardous Material Information System and some orientation topics.

The pros are that it frees up training personnel to deliver other training material that cannot be delivered via computer, such as fall-arrest training. It's also more cost effective.

WHMIS was introduced to provide information on safe use of hazardous materials in Canadian workplaces and was quite involved, requiring detailed material safety data sheets, worker education programs, and workplace labelling.

The downside of computer-based training is that it lacks the valuable interaction between student and teacher. Questions a student might have get lost, and it tends to dehumanize the whole process.

Some equipment operators don't want to take on the extra responsibility of training. Some fear they may be replaced or lose the chance of overtime once a trainee is proficient. One very good overhead crane operator agreed to train others only if he was paid at a higher rate.

There is no doubt in my mind that experienced equipment operators with good communication skills, and who have the confidence, enthusiasm and motivation, make the best trainers. As a trainer myself, it was always necessary to recognize my own limitations.

For example, I was certified to train and certify operators in the use of aerial lifts, scissor lifts, zoom booms, etc. The classroom sessions covered the legal and knowledge requirements needed to be certified. However, when it came to the practical training, although I could operate the equipment, I believed it was far more beneficial to leave it to the experts. I would act as a ground observer, which helped me out as well because I hated working from heights.

Similarly, with arc flash training, I would cover the legal, personal protective equipment and procedures but would always have a certified electrical worker cover off any technical questions.

Safety Systems, Programs, and Promotions

One of challenges that plagues some companies in their search for a solution to accident prevention is their willingness to try any new safety program, system or promotion. There seems to be a never-ending supply of initiatives to choose from. Probably the one that has had the longest run, The Neil George Safety System, is credited with dramatically improving the mining industry's accident frequency rates in many mines throughout Canada.

Other examples are PASS (positive attitude safety system), Take Five, Visible Felt Leadership, and DNV's Loss Control program… and the list goes on. Some of them come and go, some linger on painfully, others seem like a good idea at the time, but all are treated with suspicion by the general workforce. DNV or DET NORSKE VERITAS, is a very reputable, international safety rating system that assesses companies on various elements of their health and safety management systems.

Elements included in assessments are such things as leadership training, accident investigations, emergency preparedness, hiring and placement, and group communications. Levels of accomplishment are awarded by external auditors on an annual basis. The goal of achievement would be to be awarded a Level 10. Few companies worldwide have ever achieved that honour. In 2003 HBM&S was awarded a Level 7.

In 2004, Hudbay moved to a different assessment program and became certified to Occupational Health and Safety Assessment Series Management System 18001:1999. It is very prestigious for a company to hold such certification and Hudbay Minerals Inc., formerly Hudson Bay Mining and Smelting, held certification in ISO 9001:2000 for production and supply of copper anodes from molten blister copper, and ISO 14001:1996 certification for environmental compliance to the standard. To hold ISO certification in all three standards: Health and Safety, Quality Assurance, and Environmental Protection, is considered a remarkable achievement.

CORE, or Certificate of Recognition, is an occupational health and safety program designation verifying that a company has fully implemented a health and safety management system that meets national standards. When bidding on a tender or contract for work, companies and government look for this certification from the bidder in determining suitability. Some government contracts now require the contractor to be CORE certified.

One thing all such programs have in common is that they are usually brought in and sustained by senior management, sometimes lacking the support of the workers, the very people they are meant to protect.

Front-line supervisors also have a hard time with these programs because they usually mean more meetings and paperwork, or both. The supervisors then inadvertently influence the receptiveness of their crews with their own negativity toward the new initiatives.

There has always been a leaning toward change, and change is good because, again, insanity is to continue doing the same things while expecting different results. If we end up with the conclusion after somebody is badly injured that there is absolutely nothing we can change that would have affected the outcome, shame on us!

Visibly felt leadership targets the higher levels of management to spend more time in the trenches visiting the troops, so to speak. This was a way to take the pulse of the organization at ground level, to demonstrate that management cared about the everyday work taking place on its behalf. It was a simple concept.

However, it's fair to say that, at first, both management and workers felt uncomfortable with the concept and close interaction even though it had great potential. After all, who could argue with a manager or VP taking a personal interest in the day-to-day activities that were keeping the place running?

Part of the conversations that took place at the time centred around what was going well and what could be improved upon. This gave the worker an opportunity to convey ideas or concerns directly to someone who might have the power and authority to make positive changes.

Unfortunately, flavours of the month can consume a lot of dollars. Everyone involved needs to be made aware of their purpose, which includes training and information roll outs at crew meetings.

One of the issues that has a detrimental effect on any health and safety program is the bonus system that rewards employees based on production. This is particularly true when the bonus is disproportionate to the hourly rate that employees would normally earn. It leads to shortcuts and improper or improvised work standards, and it is rewarded by meeting production targets and lucrative pay cheques.

Bonus systems reinforce the belief that you can work unsafely and get the job done without getting hurt. Most of the time, that is probably true. We seldom get punished for taking shortcuts; we get rewarded instead! People often choose to do things the wrong way and never suffer the consequences. It will never happen to me, we tell ourselves. It's always the other person that suffers a serious injury.

That philosophy is one of the biggest challenges that building a safe workplace and a safe workforce has to overcome. A worker was tragically killed when climbing an escape ladder in a slag tunnel. As he climbed, the lip of the moving slag pot crushed his midsection between the ladder and the slag tunnel wall.

A couple of seconds in timing either way and he would have been spared. Unfortunately for him and his family, that was not what happened. The ladder had been used numerous times in the past without consequence, which, of course, reinforced its use.

Horses for courses, but don't always saddle a willing horse. Having said that, sometimes the willing horse gets saddled more because of its proven ability to get the job done. Some employees should not be saddled at all. Not everyone has the same tolerance for certain work.

Students are a good example. In my day, they were hired for the summer months and made a good wage replacing regular employees on vacation. It's still a good win-win and most of the general workforce embraces the opportunity to work alongside students and keep a watchful eye on them.

In one situation, however, a student went from being a bubbly, confident individual to a shell of his former self. The problem was that he had been assigned to work at heights for the summer and was petrified. He hadn't told anyone of his dilemma because he thought he might lose his job, along with the valuable funding he needed to help him through his next term at university.

Each day became a nightmare for him until he finally fessed up when challenged about how dreadful he looked. He was reassigned to a ground job, but a very valuable lesson was learned.

It wouldn't do if everyone shared the same fears, or aspirations, for that matter. Sometimes we must put the skinny guy in the tight, confined space while his buddy with the larger frame stands guard outside.

Statistically, summer students, as with all young employees, are the most vulnerable to having accidents at work for several reasons, lack of experience being just one.

One of my assignments over the past number of years was to carry out exit interviews with as many students as possible. The premise was that summer students had a unique opportunity to give the company feedback on its strengths and weaknesses – a snapshot of the organization over a three-month period by an unbiased party.

The students' comments and suggestions remained anonymous and had no bearing on whether they would get rehired the following summer. We had some great feedback over the years that suggested some students had had very positive experiences that would stay with them for a lifetime. We also learned that some issues, if not brought to light, would fester and get worse.

Some examples included bullying by one of the employees who saw summer students as fresh meat to inflict his misguided sarcasm and whit upon… and a supervisor who needed tuning up when asked by one of the students who wore prescription safety glasses if he could have a pair of prescription glasses and frames made available to fit inside a full-face respirator.

This wasn't just a reasonable request it was far more than that! Going without the glasses, which were required by prescription, was like asking someone with restricted vision to get behind the wheel of a vehicle.

The work the student was being assigned to called for a full-face respirator. He was to work inside an autoclave, a large pressure vessel similar in shape to a submarine with very restricted entry and exit points. It is probably one of the worst, if not the worst, confined space you can imagine.

The supervisor's reply to the request was to hold his hand within inches of the students face and say, "How far do you need to see."

He was also notorious for repeating a question that a student might have by sarcastically repeating it back to him, usually in a group setting. That's how most bullies operate. They need an audience in order to feed their own egos.

Summer students, usually sons and daughters of mine employees, are a valuable resource to draw on. They are usually assigned entry-level positions, which, in turn, allows full-time employees to fill more senior positions. That, then, gives employees with some time under their belts a chance for some well-deserved summer vacation. The work also eases the burden of costs associated with obtaining a university education.

However, just like regular employees, students are exposed to, and can fall victim to, the countless hazards that lurk in any work environment if they are not given the right amount of training and preparedness.

An initiative that we tried one year with a summer-student intake of 60, which seemed like a good idea at the time, was to write a letter to their parents/guardians at the start of their employment. The letter recommended they ask their wards how things were going for them at work, did they feel they had received sufficient training, were the hazards of the work they had been assigned properly identified to them, had they received the proper personal protective equipment, and did they have any issues or concerns, etc.

The letter contained the phone number of a confidential hotline that could be used by the students, guardians who were asked to leave details of any concerns raised so they could be properly addressed. We anticipated that we might get an opportunity to improve through this initiative. The result was surprising because the feedback we received was zero! Not one phone call or one note came back indicating any concerns.

Again, it seemed like a good idea but for some reason, the conversation around the supper table about the daily work activities of summer students did not raise any red flags.

I once asked an acquaintance in his late 50s how he managed to lose the ends of two of his fingers. He told me that when he was nine, he was helping his dad in his workshop. When his dad switched off the circular saw he was using the youngster hadn't realized something could still be spinning around and yet look like it wasn't moving. He reached out and touched what he thought was a stationary blade. In an instant the tops of two of his fingers were gone. It happened so suddenly his father had had no time to react.

And so it is with new employees and students. Even the simplest of tasks need to be demonstrated and clear. It may look easy for somebody who has been doing it for years, and some people learn faster than others, but never take anything for granted.

Training can take an enormous amount of time and resources. We can waste both if we don't provide the training when it is necessary and when the person receiving it is going to use it.

A new head frame and man hoist were due to be commissioned. A great amount of time and effort were put into the training of miners to be able to use the small man hoist when it came into service. Training started over three months ahead of the hand-over date when the hoist would become part of the operation, to allow the couple of hundred employees who were expected to use it a reasonable schedule to get everyone trained.

A very valuable lesson was learned when shortly after the man hoist became operational, a miner failed to open the man gate to exit at a level. While frantically trying to open the gate, he stepped onto an eight-inch ledge on the inside of the gate to try to get more leverage. As he perched on that ledge, still struggling to open the gate, the man hoist timed out and went into self-park above him and the level he was standing on.

He was then exposed to the open shaft behind him and the gate in front of him prevented him from exiting the level. If he had been a larger man, he would have been crushed by the hoist as it passed by him on the way to its park position.

Still struggling to open the gate, he realized he had forgotten to flip the gate's safety latch that prevents it from being inadvertently opened. He finally managed to move the safety latch and the gate opened, allowing him to step out onto the level and to safety.

Another employee observed him coming through the open gate with no hoist cage behind him. He reported the incident and it was promptly investigated. Had the incident not been reported, someone else might have made a similar mistake but with a far worse outcome.

A few contributing factors allowed this incident to occur. The safety latch was not easy to identify as it was corroded and blended into the rest of the hoist framework.

Hence, it was painted bright orange to improve its visibility.

It had been over three months since the miner had received training on how to operate the hoist. This was his first opportunity to put the training into practice – far too long for anyone to be expected to remember every detail of an operating procedure. Training needs to be tailored and used on a regular basis. If we train somebody for a particular task and they don't use or rarely have to perform that task, we should ask ourselves why we bother to train them at all.

In this case, rather than have over 200 employees trained to operate the man hoist who may only have to do so on rare occasions, far better to have a smaller number of trained persons operating it on a regular basis for those who are not trained.

Another dilemma that sometimes occurs when providing training is due in part to the progression lines that have been agreed to by the company and union. When employees for plant operating positions get hired, they invariable start off at the bottom, entry-level positions that require a lot of physical work. Clean up of conveyor belt lines of spillages would be one good example. The term "bull gang" is used to describe the crews that do these tasks.

As employees at the top of the seniority progression line retire quit or move to another department, everyone below them moves up the line to take the vacant position created. Advantages to this system include rewarding the senior employee with a more responsible position, higher rate of pay, and less physical demands.

It also shows the junior employee some light at the end of the tunnel so he can see he is not going to spend the rest of his life shoveling rock and concentrate. And it gives employees valuable experience of all aspects of the operation.

But with every system, there are always some flaws. Some employees can become trapped in the entry positions for much longer periods due to low turnover of manpower within a department or by transfers in above them of more senior employees from other departments.

Alternatively, when there is a higher than average turnover of labour within a department, junior employees can move rapidly through the progression lines and not have a chance to gain the experience they need at lower levels.

To facilitate the whole process, employees have to be trained, not only to do the work they are assigned within the progression line, but also on the next position they are expected to fill in order to cover for vacation relief, sickness, etc. Except, if the person at the level above doesn't need any time off for a while, the training that has been provided to the relief person becomes eroded by the winds of time.

To illustrate, an employee spends three months on the bull gang and starts to make a move up the progression list within his department. One of the new duties he is expected to perform is to operate a Bobcat or Skid Steer. He gets the training and becomes certified to operate the equipment. As with many pieces of equipment that people are trained to use, proficiency comes with experience and "seat time."

However, if seat time happens only occasionally, it can take some time to gain the necessary experience. When the employee finally assumes the new position, he might not retain it very long because the next position on the progression list opens and he moves on.

That new position may well not require him to operate a Skid Steer at all. The result is that you have lots of employees having received valuable training in the operation of equipment they have little experience with, and that they may never operate again.

Some equipment operators are reluctant to admit they can't carry out an assignment, so they try to muddle their way through it. Such was the case when a young man working for another company on site was asked to drive a front-end loader to the workshop to have lifting forks fitted. Instead of telling his supervisor he needed a little more training and experience, he jumped on the loader and subsequently ended up driving it into a creek, flipping it over onto its side as it entered the water.

Fortunately, he escaped uninjured, but it could have been much worse. Quick action at the scene also prevented an environmental impact from the equipment's hydraulic, engine and battery fluids.

Another important lesson was learned during the investigation of the loader-in-the-creek incident. Just how do you qualify an operator to drive such equipment? After all, you don't need a driver's licence, and that equipment comes in all shapes and sizes.

This is where maintaining good training records is so important. Logging the supervised training hours that a person spends on each piece of equipment is critical in being able to establish due diligence in the event of an accident, particularly if someone has been seriously injured or killed.

As an operator demonstrates proficiency on each piece of mobile equipment, a declaration should be placed in his training file giving the date and signatures of his supervisor and himself and stating that the operator had demonstrated sufficient ability to operate the equipment.

Some owners may be reluctant to "certify" their equipment operators and hand them the necessary credentials as proof of competency. This is sometimes born out of fear of losing the operator to a competitor after they have taken the time and trouble to train them. This is also true of some contractors, who refuse to release training records to employees who leave their service.

Influences, Errors and Omissions

The Ravens

Safety is a serious business. You cannot have a sense of humour when someone has been hurt. However, as you can imagine, humorous moments that don't hurt anyone have occurred along the way. A couple of them involved ravens.

Garbage dumpsters around company property were being picked through by ravens for leftover food that had been tossed in garbage bags by lunchroom cleaning staff.

When the safety committee got involved, the first thought was to cover the dumpsters with steel lids. The dumpsters were emptied by picking them up with a front-end loader and dumping the contents into the back of a large truck. The steel lids would have to be heavy and substantial enough to withstand a good beating because the dumpster was often shaken by the front-end loader to be sure all the contents found its way into the back of the truck.

One of the committee members mentioned that the local curling club he was involved with had covered their air intake vents on the outside of the building with black garbage bags to stop air flowing into the building when they didn't need it.

However, the ravens would peck holes in the bags, so they had to keep replacing them. Black garbage bags weren't available one day, so they used orange ones instead. Low and behold, the ravens left the orange garbage bags alone. Orange bags are usually used for leaves and garden refuge, and no one has ever seen a raven attempt to rip apart an orange bag of leaves.

We decided to try an experiment before we invested in new lids for the dumpsters. We asked the cleaning staff in one area to use orange garbage bags for food waste from the lunchrooms instead of the regular black bags before putting them in the dumpster.

After two weeks, none of the orange garbage bags in the dumpsters had been disturbed by the ravens. It was amazing! Who would have thought the problem could be solved as easily as changing the colour of disposal bags to fool the birds. The two-week experiment seemed to have been successful so I issued a plant-wide notice stating that in future all lunchrooms would use orange garbage bags for food disposal.

However, the day after the notice went out, things returned to normal. It was almost as if the ravens had read my notice and figured out that they had been fooled. So much for trying to outsmart them. We went with steel and heavy nylon lids a short time later. The story amused many around the plant.

Garbage was not the only issue we had with ravens, which, by the way, were referred to by some in northern

Manitoba as Thompson turkeys because they are always plentiful in that northern city. The main north head frame was demolished, and a truck ramp was built to enable ore to be brought to the ore bins at the Flin Flon crusher. Ravens decided that the steelwork structure of the ramp made a perfect resting place.

Unfortunately, they also liked to poop when resting and an electrical transformer close by was taking a direct hit. A plastic (dead) raven was hung from the ramp to get the rest of them to reconsider their new retreat but that didn't work!

However, a solution was found for the excremental problem. Steel spikes where welded close together on the beams that were being used as perches. This was the new reality the birds where confronted with – a kind of bed of nails! Man's ingenuity had prevailed at last.

Workplace Culture

When workers get their first employment opportunity they are usually exited, keen, and willing. What happens to them within a very short time is that their attitude more and more resembles that of the personnel they are working with. If the rest of the workforce is happy, the new workers tend to be happy. If the workforce is intolerant and complacent, then they too can be swallowed up by that culture, or whatever culture exists within the organization.

Organizational culture is subtle. It does not change over the short term. It reflects the way a company manages its business and is created from within; it can't be mandated. It can have a positive or negative effect on the way people work. It can be measured by morale, high turnover, absenteeism, and accident frequency rates. It can also be measured by the number of grievances filed, and the amount of discipline handed out.

Organizational culture reflects "the way we do business around here." For example, there may be a lot of rules that need to be followed at Company X, but they are seldom enforced. Hence, many employees believe those rules are not important and don't need to be followed all the time.

Employees may follow a rule, not so much because they see value in it but more to appease. They are compliant. They don't wish to rock the boat. Some employees, on the other hand, like to push the envelope. They don't see any point in following a rule that is inconsistently enforced.

Company X has a clean shaving policy for anyone required to work in a respirator-required area. Work areas have been identified by industrial hygiene monitoring to determine this requirement. All employees working in those areas must have no facial hair below the bottom lip. It's an important rule.

It's also a Canadian Standards Association standard to have a respiratory-fit test to ensure a proper seal, which is also part of the Workplace Health and Safety Act. Most employees comply, a few grow a little stubble, some sprout patches between their bottom lip and chin, and some allow their moustaches to droop below their bottom lip.

Enter the new CEO on his first tour of duty. He notices that some of the employees on his tour have facial hair in all the wrong places. Upon ending his tour, he sends out emails to the department heads and supervisors of the employees involved. The message is simple: Please provide me with an explanation as to how this obvious rule is being allowed to be broken.

It might seem to be an easy question to answer but if you are a supervisor or a manager that has allowed this set of circumstances to exist, it's not so easy. Needless to say, somebody is going to get a shave, and others are going to get their asses kicked.

It's a lot easier for the new guy on the block to address issues of noncompliance than for a CEO who has allowed the deviations to exist and fester on his watch.

Note to new supervisors and department heads: What you allow, you approve! Don't just talk the talk. Walk the walk! Set yourself and work crews up to be successful by ensuring work is being performed the way it is supposed to be done. Don't compromise yourself and others by turning a blind eye. You can quickly gain the respect of your personnel and you can just as quickly lose it.

Errors

After a drug and alcohol awareness training session I was presenting one day, a night shift supervisor took me to one side after the training had wrapped up. He shared with me an experience that he had had with one of his crew members, who had come to work one night impaired.

Rather than arrange for him to get home safely and let him know that the matter would be discussed with him when he was sober, the supervisor decided to give him a break and told the other members of the crew to keep an eye on him until he was okay to be left alone.

A couple of nights later, the same employee reported for work in even worse shape than he had a few shifts before. The situation escalated because it had not been addressed. The supervisor finally did what he should have done the first time around. Unfortunately, he had compromised himself and others the first time and had sent a message to his crew that he was prepared to tolerate that kind of behaviour. You don't get second chances to do the right thing first time around.

Many supervisors don't appreciate the influence they have over their subordinates. This can be shown in a number of ways, from general housekeeping to PPE and rule compliance. A supervisor constantly sends out subtle messages about what he will tolerate.

Traits of good supervision are consistency, fairness, respect for others, and appreciation. Throw in being knowledgeable and having good communication skills and you have a person for whom you would probably like to work. A supervisor has nailed it if his or her crew works in the same way whether that supervisor is present or not.

For a supervisor to do the right thing all the time can be tough to nearly impossible, but especially if he or she is undermined by other supervisors who are not prepared to tackle difficult situations, like rule enforcement.

When workers see a bar that is constantly changing, they become confused and dissatisfied. Rules that are applied inconsistently by various members of the management team or levels of supervision create heroes and villains. Unfortunately, all too often the villain is the supervisor who mans up and deals with the issues that confront him rather than choosing to look the other way or ignore issues entirely.

When a rule is being violated, some supervisors find it hard to leave an established comfort zone between them and their subordinates, particularly if they have chosen in the past to nurture the human relationship rather than deal with similar issues. You can't suddenly start enforcing rules with people who are used to your not enforcing them.

Such a situation is not unlike raising children. If one parent provides the authority and discipline while the other lets things slide, a very unhealthy environment can be created.

Discipline is a tough tool to use in any workplace. It can sour relationships, particularly if it is used inconsistently or unfairly. I'm not suggesting discipline should not be used but it should be a last resort. Many supervisors feel they get hung out to dry when they apply discipline only to see it overturned after a grievance hearing.

Human Resources blames the supervisor for not properly documenting progressive discipline and the supervisor blames HR for its lack of support.

The supervisor may also be undermined by senior members of his own crew, particularly when it comes to new safety initiatives. It's hard to teach an old dog new tricks, particularly when the old dogs are close to retirement and feel they are bulletproof, and also have the benefit of a union to go to bat for them should they get themselves into trouble.

When supervisors do administer discipline, they can expect pushback. When one rule is applied, expect all to apply. The expression "work to rule" came out of this type of environment.

Creating a workplace where everyone is happy, productive, and safe is a tough challenge. These things go hand in hand. An unhappy workforce is less productive and more prone to accidents. Worker morale plays a big factor in workplace health and safety.

So how can a supervisor appease his crew while still enforcing rules and safety requirements? One answer to this question is to make sure workers understand that their supervisor may be held accountable for their actions. In the event of a serious injury, the supervisor comes under intense scrutiny to ensure that he had assigned work the employee could perform. The supervisor also must demonstrate that the injured employee was aware of any hazards and was suitably protected from those hazards to avoid injury.

A case in point: A maintenance supervisor is driving back to his area's workshop after attending his morning production meeting. It's about 1.5 hours into the shift, just before morning coffee. He is surprised to see an ambulance pulling away from the area. He is also surprised by the fact that it is carrying one of the members of his crew.

More surprises follow. One of the first questions to other members of his crew is what happened and why was the ambulance called? He is told that one of his guys had fallen from a ladder in the shop and it looked like he may have broken his wrist.

"What was he doing up a ladder?" the supervisor asks.

"Retrieving a proximity switch off the top of the heater in the stock room," is the answer.

"What proximity switch, and why was it on top of the heater?"

It was the proximity switch that the boom of the lineman's bucket truck sits on when it's properly parked in its down travel position. In winter, it sometimes freezes up and, even though the boom is correctly parked, a warning light is displayed on the dashboard of the truck indicating that it is still in the raised position.

The normal procedure when an operating problem occurs with a piece of equipment is to notify the supervisor. The supervisor then determines what action is required. In this case, the action required would be to issue a repair work order to the garage to have the problem rectified. If necessary, the truck would be taken out of service until it had been fixed.

In a previous experience with the same issue, the injured employee had seen what the mechanic in the garage had done at the time to rectify the problem. After all, it involved only a couple of screws, unplugging the unit, and allowing the switch to thaw in a warm environment.

The injured employee, without being instructed to do so, had decided to carry out the repair himself. That is how the proximity switch ended up on top of a heater in the stock room and how an employee sustained a broken wrist, all without his supervisor's knowledge.

In some respects, you could acknowledge the employee for showing some initiative in saving time by carrying the repair out himself. On the other hand, having a serious injury result from performing work that had not been assigned negates all good intentions. Workers need to be constantly reminded that their supervisor needs to know where they are and what they are doing. They should also know that any change to the scope of work they are performing must be approved by their superior, unless they have received prior authorization to the contrary.

Government inspectors typically focus their attention on the supervisor when they observe rule violations because they see the supervisor as the one with control over the workplace and the employees. It is essential that someone fulfill that role, otherwise everything falls apart under the grand scheme of things. It's called accountability. It's what ultimately may lead to a supervisor being answerable for his actions or decisions at an inquiry or inquest into a workplace fatality.

The supervisor's due diligence will be measured in the training, observation, work procedures, and any inspection records he is able to produce. This, in turn, demonstrates that he had assigned work to employees who were competent to perform that work and knew full well the hazards associated with it, as well as the correct methods of mitigating those hazards.

One of the consequences of the smelter explosion and the resulting inquiry was that it highlighted the need to ensure this was happening.

A pushback came from some workers through acknowledging they had been made aware of potential hazards through safety contacts and their signatures on attendance sheets. Some workers refused to sign the acknowledgement for fear they would be held more accountable in the event of any future serious event.

Another pushback came when a "Take Five" program was introduced that required an employee to complete a record card before starting work. The purpose of the record card was to demonstrate that the worker had taken the time beforehand to assess the hazards he was going to be exposed to before starting a task. They were also meant to identify the necessary controls they had chosen to use.

An example could be that an employee might identify the potential for dust inhalation. The controls might be to turn on ventilation fans, have the area cleaned, and wear a respirator.

Many people believe such a measure takes responsibility away from supervisors, so they are not responsible for any hazard or risk assessment. The responsibility is everyone's! Supervisors are not supermen or women. They may have inadvertently missed something.

It is seldom that a supervisor gets hurt. Most injuries don't occur in the boardrooms or offices of corporations. Injuries occur at the point of contact or, what I like to call where the rubber meets the road.

For a worker to be asked to take five minutes before starting a task to consider if he knows what he is doing, that he has the necessary tools and equipment, and that he is aware of any hazards and necessary controls, is powerful stuff! After all, workers have the most to lose if something goes wrong. They are the ones that risk being injured, the ones who will suffer most.

I have lost track of the number of times I have interviewed injured employees who wished they could dial back the clock and take that little bit of extra time to consider the consequences of their actions. The problem is that sometimes you don't get a second chance!

Omissions

I have had many close calls throughout my career. One that I remember vividly was the first time I went underground at one of the mines. I was very fortunate to have a co-worker with me who looked out for me. We had descended to the level that we were to work on by traveling down the shaft in the hoist man cage. At that level, we opened the gate of the cage and stepped into the maintenance shop.

Our job was to remove a redundant overhead crane. During a break, curiosity got the better of me and I decided to take a closer look at the shaft that we had gotten out of a few hours earlier.

As I stuck my head over the top of the gate to see if I could see the bottom of the shaft, I felt a sharp tug on my shoulder with enough force that I was almost thrown to the ground. I looked up to see my co-worker waving his fist at me.

"If I ever catch you doing that again, I will be the one who knocks your head off."

Just then the man cage zipped by the gate en route to another level and I realized just how lucky I had been. Had I not been pulled aside by my co-worker, I would have been decapitated by the moving cage. I have often thought back to that moment and realized how lucky I was.

Since then, I have had greater respect for the expression, "Curiosity killed the cat!" I could have died right there and would never have known what happened.

I found out later that another mine employee had been killed years earlier under similar circumstances.

I was also made aware of another young worker who, on his first visit underground, had opened a shaft door and fallen to his death. After that, whenever I visited an underground mine, I always gave the mine shaft a wide berth.

But that wasn't the only time in my 49-year career that I had a near-death experience. I was once one of three workers taken to hospital when the scaffolding that we were working on collapsed. All three of us went crashing down to the bottom of the thickener that we were working on in the mill.

Luckily, we were not seriously hurt but many workers have lost their lives falling from heights far less than that. One of the saving factors in my incident was that the scaffolding boards traveled with us and gave somewhat of a cushioning effect when we hit the thick muddy bottom of the thickener.

One of the underlying causes in that incident was a miss communication at shift change. The crew ahead of us had only tack welded the scaffold supports in place.

I can also count my blessings that I came down from the smelter reverb furnace when I did the night of the explosion in Flin Flon. A few short minutes earlier, I had been at the side of the furnace, standing with two other crew members. They also came down from the furnace with me. Had we stayed just that few minutes longer the consequences would have been unimaginable.

Unfortunately, others that night were not as fortunate. The trauma that they and their families suffered will last a lifetime.

When it comes to getting injured at work, young people entering the workforce for the first time appear to be at the greatest risk. That's what the numbers tell us, and much has been written and debated about why that is. On one hand, the youth of the day are more likely to challenge and ask questions if they don't think something is the way it should be. That's the theory, but in practice it can be a different story.

Education of new workers has started in the high schools with programs such as "Young Workers of Tomorrow." I was fortunate, along with a co-worker who was a full-time union safety representative, to participate in the program. Together, we would attend schools and give presentations on workers' rights, the importance of reporting accidents, etc.

Many of our students had already entered the workforce in a part-time capacity and it was interesting to note how many had already suffered an injury and not reported it. I believe some were uncomfortable about the whole process and saw getting hurt at work as a result of something that they had done wrong.

I know from my own experience when I started my own apprenticeship in a steel works facility at 16 that I never felt vulnerable. I spent three months with the overhead crane crew as part of my training but was never worried about heights. I never wore fall protection and I would often walk the crane rails with a sheer drop on one side. As a young guy, I felt invincible.

Fast forward many years later and, call it whatever you like, I developed a fear of heights, or maybe I had matured enough to no longer believe I could never fall and hit the ground with deadly force. When I look back at my formative years, I sometimes shudder to think of what I managed to get away with.

Steel erectors used to put compelling arguments forward as to why they needed to wear running shoes and did not need to be tied off.

During the construction of the pressure leach system, which was a major project in the 90s, they did it their way. A decade later, during the construction of the head fame, 777 regulations were in place, all mandating 100 percent tie-off at all times while working at heights. That head fame was built with no issues.

The construction industry has had an appalling number of fatalities over the years, with many attributed to falls from heights. Being struck by falling objects also comes high on the list. One of the things you can't help noticing when you visit a worksite is how some workers interpret compliance.

They are obviously aware of the requirement to wear certain things, such as a fall arrest harness and lanyard. Unfortunately, they miss the point of wearing one, doing so only to appease their supervisor or the safety guy who might drop by for a visit. They wear it with reluctance. It is on, but not properly adjusted. The lanyard is too long, dangling off the edge of a roof or, even worse, it would have hit the ground before it was deployed. The anchor point to which everything else is attached, including the worker, is totally inadequate.

They just don't get it! It's not about appeasing their boss or me, or anyone else for that matter. It's all about them. Safety is personal! Putting on safety glasses or a respirator when you see your supervisor coming isn't going to protect you when you really need protection.

Workers must see the value in what they are being asked to do or wear. Too many rules that are not enforced consistently, personal protective equipment that is supplied but not worn, or is improperly adjusted or poorly maintained, create an environment that asks for trouble.

It's not just personal protective equipment compliance either. Another good example is slings used in rigging for lifting heavy items. The number of slings that are destroyed after a formal inspection is unreal. Which begs the question when they were last used, and why were they still in service?

Underground miners and tradesmen would often send equipment to the surface machine shop for repair and leave slings on the equipment. You could bet money these "gifted" slings had not been their prize possessions, or they would not have given them away. How the lifting gear had managed to survive the journey from the depths of the earth is unreal.

It wasn't as if there was a shortage of this type of equipment. The mine spent a small fortune each year on slings and associated hardware. It was that some people just didn't want to part with the good stuff that they had stashed away for special occasions.

Another issue we had both above ground and underground was seatbelt compliance. Seatbelts were part of the Golden Rules of Vehicle Safety that seemed to meet a lot of resistance from many employees, particularly in a loading bay where workers had to constantly get on and off the forklifts. They were never in their seats on the equipment for any more than five minutes at a time, sometimes even less than that.

Operators suffered constant aggravation having to belt up. They saw little value in doing so, particularly when they were operating on smooth cement floors at relatively low speeds. Some even buckled up the seatbelt when their forklift was unoccupied so they could just jump into their seat and drive away, the offending belt tucked underneath them and out of sight.

They even muscled up enough support from sympathetic supervisors that they wrote to the Mines Inspection Branch to ask for an exemption from wearing seatbelts while performing this type of work. The request was denied. Rules are rules and you can seldom convince a government body to bend them, even when the argument may be compelling.

It's possible to work around these issues but sometimes that can be expensive. For instance, there are forklifts that require the operator to stand rather than sit when operating the machine, which negates the requirement for having to wear a seatbelt. It also reduces the cumulative effect of having to mount and dismount the machine to a standing/sitting position 30-40 times a day.

Similarly, some workers were prone to ignore seatbelts while operating internal surface vehicles. Again, the excuse offered by many was short distances at low speeds.

Seatbelts in the surface eight-seater van used to transport workers to their work locations were always a bone of contention also. This was particularly true in the winter when the occupants wore heavy winter parkers. It was a struggle to get in and out of the van and into a vacant seat. Attempting to buckle up once seated just added to the challenge. It seemed that just when you managed to get all settled, and in compliance with the necessary requirements, you had arrived at your destination.

Again, an exemption seemed a reasonable request. After all, taxis and school buses don't have to meet the seatbelt rule. However, the fact remains, seatbelts are like every other piece of safety equipment. You never know just when they are going to be needed.

One of the reasons why their use was included in the golden rules of vehicle safety was because an Anglo passenger van rolled off a highway in South Africa. That incident contributed to the high number of fatalities that Anglo sustained that year.

In a vehicle incident on the mine's surface site that was much closer to home, a van carrying three passengers on a night shift struck a rail line with its sub frame. The van wasn't travelling very fast, but the abrupt stop sent its unrestrained, unsuspecting occupants flying forward, resulting in a cautionary hospital visit to get checked out.

The only member of the crew who had a seatbelt on was the supervisor who was driving them to their workstations. The impact of the van striking the rail line was so severe that it resulted in the vehicle being written off.

On another occasion, an employee who drove a company delivery truck for the mine failed to stop at an internal rail crossing. The close call was reported by the train crew. One outcome from a subsequent review of the incident by the driver's manager was that he had to attend a meeting with me. The purpose was so that he would receive a one-on-one, documented safety contact on the hazards and rules around such crossings.

I could not help smiling a few days later when I observed a sign in the delivery truck's rear window that read, "I stop at all crossings".

I can only recall two or three incidents when a vehicle and a locomotive struck each other. Fortunately, nobody was injured in either case. We received countless reports, however, of near-miss incidents at many of the unprotected rail crossings throughout the surface operations.

Locomotives were used for any number of things, such as hauling molten slag pots, concentrates, ore from the mine, coal and oil to feed the furnaces, shipping zinc and copper products to market, etc. Our surface plant was a maze of rail tracks running in almost every direction from one end to the other. The rail trestle at the main entrance to the plant is a landmark, directly opposite the guard shack.

The first incident involved two shift workers, one on an afternoon shift and the other on the night shift. They were on a hot change, which meant, one could not leave the plant until his relief took over.

The night shift worker drove his "cross shift" in a company vehicle to a drop off point close to his vehicle in the company employee parking lot. Unfortunately, on this particular evening, they stopped to chat on a little-used rail crossing close to the parking lot. I say "unfortunately" because a locomotive pushing a load of railcars came down the track and pushed them along sideways for about 50 yards before everything came to rest.

The truck was bent like a banana with the two occupants still inside, shaken up but otherwise unhurt. It proved to be a good reminder to everyone that unmanned rail crossings are no place to stop and shoot the breeze.

To increase awareness of the close calls that were being reported by our train and track crew, our chief plant protection officer at the time and myself had a tow truck bring in an almost brand-new half ton truck from the local wrecker's yard. The truck was a total write-off after a highway accident. We had it placed on the rail line that ran just outside the main change house at the time. We also had a rail car left on the track and butted the truck up against it. All this was done under cover of darkness when nobody was around.

The following morning, as the day shift employees exited the change house enroute to the plant to start their shift and the night shift went to the change house at the end of their shift, they all could not avoid seeing the apparent carnage. We let the rumour mill, company grapevine, and local coffee shop do the rest. There was no Internet or social media in those days.

As news of the truck's demise spread, news of the occupant's condition was greatly exaggerated, especially as there had been no occupants in the vehicle to begin with. Fake news? Yes! Effective? Yes! We experienced a lower reporting rate of rail crossing near misses, at least for a little while.

I was once called to the scene of a single-vehicle accident in which a large vacuum truck was lying on its side. This occurred on the mine site, but the truck was owned by a contractor and its operator was a contract employee. The vacuum truck had been driven a little too close to the soft shoulder on the roadway and you could see by the tire marks how it had been drawn away from its intended route.

The investigation revealed that although the operator was trained and had a licence to operate that class of vehicle, unfortunately, that licence had expired and had not been renewed. That meant the cost of the repairs to the vehicle, which were considerable, was born by the contractor.

One lesson learned from that incident was to be sure any operator of a licensed company vehicle has maintained current status. If, for any reason, their licence is revoked, they must notify their supervisor and HR immediately.

Fortunately, no injuries were sustained as a result of the incident, in part because the vehicle operator was wearing a seatbelt.

In another vehicle incident a large tandem ore truck had left the highway shortly after the start of a two-hour journey. The resulting investigation revealed that the driver had placed his sandwiches and a thermos of coffee for his trip next to him on the passenger seat. The seal on the thermos was subject to leaking if not placed in an upright position.

As he steered the truck around a bend in the highway, the thermos shifted to a horizontal position so, fearing that his sandwiches were about to be soaked in coffee, the driver was momentarily distracted as he reached out to correct the situation. When he returned his attention to the road, it was no longer in sight. That's how quickly you can turn a good day into a bad one!

Many deadly sins exist when it comes to causes of accidents. Distraction and inattentiveness, anger and frustration, ego, boredom, being rushed, complacency and routine, fatigue, and a sense of invincibility are all potential contributing factors in many accidents. This list is not all inclusive and it doesn't suggest blame. There are a lot of reasons why these sins come up. Many are created by the environment in which people find themselves.

People are human and it is the human element of safety that is the most challenging and intriguing. We all take risks, some more than others, but I am sure you will agree, we have all experienced the emotions or states of mind mentioned above from time to time in no particular order and, no doubt, we always will.

Being aware and accepting the fact that they all contribute in some way or another to a great many accidents can be beneficial. Some of the latest motor vehicles have sensors that monitor the driver's actions. For example, if the vehicle wanders from its intended path a couple of times over a short period of time, a coffee cup is displayed on the dashboard, suggesting it might be time for the driver to pull over and take a break.

Distracted driving in Ontario has now replaced alcohol-impaired driving as the No. 1 cause of automobile fatalities.

When workers feel under pressure to rush or hurry, whether it's imposed on them from outside or self-imposed, their risk of being injured rises.

Ego certainly claims its victims as well, especially when workers feel they will be thought less of if they either ask for physical help, such as, "Can you give me a hand to lift this?" or not physical, such as, "I am not quite sure how to do this part of the job. I've never done it before."

This is particularly true of young people entering the workforce, and of older employees, both of whom don't want to show vulnerability. If we are angry or frustrated the situation is in danger of getting worse through a consequential injury.

Some workers can become so adept at doing a task that they become absent minded, almost transfixed. They go through the motions and could literally do the task blindfolded. Driving the same route day after day to get to work, for instance. It's only when something unanticipated breaks that momentum that they are brought back to reality.

Not everyone can earn an income at a job with which they feel completely satisfied and happy. When you are lucky enough to be in a position that gives you enjoyment, it is no longer "work."

Many years ago, a friend's son struggled as he neared the end of high school with what he wanted to do for the rest of his life. At 16 and 17 that's a tough decision to make. I know my own career path was mapped out for me when I failed my "eleven-plus" exam.

In the United Kingdom in the 60s and 70s, that exam separated students into two groups Either pass the exam and go on to a grammar school education and university to become a doctor, lawyer, teachers, etc., or fail and go into the auto plants as operators, the construction industry as labourers, or into the trades.

Posters in career offices showed a person in a cap and gown beside a person in coveralls. The caption underneath read, "Work Smarter, not Harder!"

Many people today believe the poster was totally wrong. If anything, it should have read. "Work Smart and Hard."

There is nothing wrong with choosing either career path. In fact, in many cases, the person depicted in the coveralls as a tradesman does very well. Tradesmen have always been in demand, are seldom out of work, and make a very good income, unlike some of their university-grad counterparts, who enter the workforce with education debt.

By virtue of the fact they have qualifications but lack experience. university grads can also have difficulty getting hired. Underground miners, on the other hand, who may lack a grounded education, can still make more money in a year than a university college professor.

My friend's son who was trying to pick a career path, finally came home and announced to his parents that he knew what he wanted to do for the rest of his life. He wanted to be a greenskeeper at a golf course. And, I might add, there is absolutely nothing wrong with choosing such a profession. It's a great job, particularly in the UK where the golf courses are open year-round.

Part of the training involves attending horticultural college and learning landscaping and drainage technics. You get to work in beautiful surroundings, a friendly atmosphere, and the pay is not bad. I have a nephew who has made a good career out of doing the same thing.

After being employed as an apprentice grounds keeper for about a year, a job that our friends fully supported, their son became a shadow of his former self. He retreated to his room only to surface at mealtimes. He was quiet, withdrawn, and never got involved in family conversations. His parents became increasingly worried about him as the days passed into months.

Finally, his mother had had enough. She confronted her son to find out what was wrong. Why was he so withdrawn? He finally broke down and came out from behind his mask.

"I hate being a greenskeeper," he said.

The penny finally dropped with his parents. His mother said she could have guessed as much, recalling how she had never been able to get her son even to cut the front lawn or do any yard work at all. That fact alone should have been enough for her to warn him that greens keeping might not be the best career path for him.

Her son gave up on being a greenskeeper. Instead, he became a very happy, prosperous furniture salesman. Fortunately for him, he had only "wasted" a little over a year of his life.

I have seen many employees who have spent a lifetime in jobs they were either not cut out for or were totally miserable in. They lacked the will, initiative, or financial security to move on and try something they might have found more fulfilling.

I felt bad one morning when I walked into work and offered a "Good morning" to one of the guys who happened to be walking through the main gate at the same time.

"What's good about it?" he replied. "I've got another 12 years of putting up with this crap before I retire."

Hardly a good start to anyone's day!

One of the summer students a few years ago was assigned to work with the paint crew. He soon became withdrawn, not his usual bubbly self. I found out that his condition was brought on by the fact he was mortified working at heights.

For the first few weeks of his employment, everything had gone well, until he was assigned to work up in the rafters scraping paint off the beams and putting on a fresh coat.

He had not told anyone about his fear of working at heights because he thought doing so might prematurely end his employment. So, every day he came to work and lived a nightmare. He lost his appetite, couldn't sleep, and became pretty distraught. When he finally admitted his fear to me, he was near to becoming a total wreck.

The situation was quickly resolved. His work assignment was changed to enable his feet to remain firmly on the ground and he was grateful for the opportunity to continue working. After all, he was a hard-working young man who fell into a trap that a lot of young workers fall into and then sometimes suffer the consequences of an injury, and a lifetime of regret for failing to speak up.

I once read an information pamphlet on advising young workers about appropriate questions to ask a prospective employer in a job interview, such as: What training will I receive? What hazards on the job will I be exposed to? How will I be expected to protect myself?

All good stuff but, unfortunately, it has been my experience that young people sometimes accept a job not even knowing what their pay will be. They are so excited to have a job interview and then the subsequent job offer that they don't want to muddy the waters by asking a whole bunch of questions.

An employee was once a little upset that his work assignment was to crawl into a receiving tank to clean the inside walls and repaint them. It was what is commonly called "a confined space." His beef was that out of his three-man crew, he was the one always assigned to crawl into the tank through a small opening while his mates remained outside. The work was hot and dirty.

The reason he was always "the chosen one" was because he was the only one who could fit through the opening in the tank, and physically fit enough to endure the work. His view was that just because he kept himself in good physical shape he shouldn't have to end up in the tank every time.

Hopefully, his supervisor took note of his dilemma and gave him a break on some other tough assignments that his compadres were more capable of performing.

Tough jobs exist in the mine and surface operations. Some can test the heart and soul of anyone. Can you imagine being on a clean-up crew when on every shift there is a pile of spillage from a conveyor belt to clean up? The only way it can be removed is to shovel it by hand back onto the belt. It takes you the best part of your shift to get it done and put the area back to what it should be.

You come back the next shift and it's just like being in the movie *Ground Hog Day*. Only sometimes even worse. The work these employees do is important. They help to keep the place running and should never be undervalued or underestimated. They can help make or break a company.

If I had been asked at that point where and under what circumstances our next serious accident would happen, I could never in my wildest dreams have predicted it, particularly since we were a mine site. The injury was a broken leg, the result of a large circular bale of straw falling from the back of a flatbed truck while it was being unloaded.

The injured employee worked for a contractor who was responsible for delivering straw to be used on the tailings pond to reduce dust when the ponds froze over in the winter months.

One of the lessons learned in the subsequent investigation was that emergency response protocols had not been followed. The two contractors involved in off-loading the straw were in a remote area of the mine site. They had made previous deliveries and had gained access to the area from a back road. The main site entrance had restricted height access because of a railway trestle just inside the main gate.

All emergency calls within the mine site went through the plant protection office at the main gate, which is manned 24/7. Personnel there, in turn, would request assistance from whatever emergency response providers were appropriate. This protocol meant they knew there was an incident on site, where it was, and its general nature.

It also allowed them to have a plant protection vehicle meet the response vehicle at the main gate and escort it to the scene. That was of particular value because the surface plant covered a large area, making it difficult to navigate if the responder was not familiar with the layout of the roads and buildings.

Unfortunately, when the bale of straw landed on the employee, his partner pulled out his cell phone and called 911. The ambulance was immediately dispatched to the main gate as per responders' protocols. The plant protection officer stationed at the main gate saw the ambulance pull up outside his window but had no idea what was going on. He also has no escort to assist. He didn't even know where the emergency was! Valuable minutes were wasted before everyone could figure out what was happening.

In the end, the injured employee was transported to the hospital and then on to Winnipeg for treatment.

The accident scene was not preserved as required under the Mines Act for an injury of this nature. Photographs taken at the scene proved invaluable in helping to determine what had taken place. Conflicting statements came from the only eyewitness and the injured person, who was not available for a thorough interview because of his hospitalization.

The area where the bails were being off loaded was not suitable because the ground was sloped and uneven, which was a contributing factor in the incident. As a result, a new designated drop off point for the straw was established and protocols for emergency contacts for contractors were strengthened.

Sometimes it's the simplest of routine tasks that can lead to devastating injuries. A contractor was removing a flexible fitting from a waste oil container and had removed his safety glasses only moments before because they were fogging up. As the fitting became free, the coupling at the end of the hose sprang back and caught him in the eye. He lost his eye as a result.

The Right to Refuse

The right to refuse is one of the cornerstones of safety legislation. It is seldom used but one of the best examples I can recall demonstrates its relevance and benefits.

The reverb furnace boiler stood almost three stories high. Occasionally, when one of the boiler's internal water tubes developed a leak during furnace operation, a repair was needed, which was a big job involving hard, dirty work. It meant emptying the furnace as much as possible but, at the same time, because it was a refractory brick furnace, it could not be allowed to completely cool off for risk of collapsing.

A water-cooled isolation damper that acts like a steel wall was then lowered into place to provide a physical barrier between the furnace and the boiler, and then the boiler was drained of all remaining water.

The next part of the job involved entering the boiler for descaling. This involved bringing down as much of the hard lumps of material that build up inside the boiler (clinkers) as possible. The boiler tubes also need to be inspected and repaired. Carpenters built internal decking, ladder-ways and bulkheads. Once that was done, high-pressure welders went in and carried out repairs to the leaking tube.

This work had been done numerous times over the years without questioning the high degree of risk involved. One of the biggest issues was entering the boiler, which could only be done from the bottom level. There was always the danger of large pieces of clinker breaking away from the side of the boiler flu walls and striking one of the workers below before a bulkhead could be put into place for protection.

The right to refuse was used by one of the powerhouse personnel who questioned the integrity and reliability of the water-filled isolation damper. What would happen if the water supply to it was shut off or failed? That was the only protection they had. How long would it take for the steel damper to melt? Should that happen, anyone inside the boiler would be exposed to the tremendous heat of the furnace.

The fact that workers had completed the task numerous times before had no bearing on satisfying this worker's concerns. He wanted answers and until such time as the company could satisfy him, he was not going inside the boiler.

The work was shut down, the mines inspector was called in after all other avenues of the right to refuse had been exhausted, and a plan was formulated to satisfy the concerns. Thermo engineers were asked to calculate how much time it would take if the water supply to the damper was to abruptly stop. How long would it take for the damper to catastrophically fail, allowing the heat from the furnace into the boiler chambers? What other circumstances could cause the damper to fail in position?

Factors such as how long the damper had been in commission, how well had it had been maintained, what was the ideal thickness of the damper's steel walls before they should be replaced were considered. Other questions were also asked.

What could cause the water supply to the damper to be suddenly lost? How soon would it be before the remaining water in the damper turned to steam and increased its vulnerability to the heat of the adjacent furnace?

Other factors that existed while the boiler was occupied by workers included vibration caused by electric rail tram cars rolling over the floor above, which were used to drop feed into the furnace below.

How were occupants of the boiler to be warned if they needed to exit in an emergency? What rescue plans needed to be in place to remove an injured worker from inside the boiler.

The list continued to grow and so did the realization that although the work had seemed routine in the past, it had been performed without consideration of the "What ifs" and, in that regard, luck rather than anything else had prevailed.

Eventually, proper procedures were written, additional training took place, and rail traffic above the furnace ceased whenever the boiler was occupied. Water to the damper was continuously monitored, isolation damper maintenance was improved, and rescue plans were tested.

The good news was that all this was accomplished not because somebody got seriously injured. A worker correctly identified a danger to himself and others and used his right to refuse to have that danger addressed.

As a footnote, the next time the reverb furnace went down for its major rebuild a couple of years later, the reverb boiler underwent significant improvements to its design, which included additional access points from the top of the boiler and stretcher doors. Provision was also made to allow protective beams to be moved into position without putting workers at undue risk.

Considerable costs came with these improvements – over $2 million – but it did demonstrate the company's strong commitment to safety. Sixty pressure welders were employed for 10 days, but that's another story.

One right-to-refuse situation that was not very well received at the time was when a worker used it when assigned work in an area of the smelter called the convertor pit. His belief was that a shift boss who had control of the area would carry out a threat to kill him if he got the chance.

The threat had been uttered earlier when they had been in an argument over something unrelated.

The worker was also a union activist and some at the company regarded the use of the "Right to Refuse" as frivolous, which could become grounds for insubordination and possible dismissal.

The refusal soon reached the ears of the government mines inspector who was asked to rule on the issue. One of lessons in the incident, and in other issues that are taken to a third party for settlement, is that you can never predict an outcome. This has been proven to me many times over the years.

My best advice to both parties engaged in a dispute is to always try to reach a compromise rather than leave your fate to an adjudicator.

The outcome in this case was in favour of the worker who had been threatened, even though the shift boss had spoken out in anger and likely would never have carried out the threat. The mines inspected ruled that a perceived threat could distract the worker while in the area, so he ordered the company to reassign the employee to another work location.

Another factor the inspector considered as part of his decision was that there had, in fact, been an employee killed by another employee some years earlier in close proximity to the work location in question. As a result, the worker then withdrew his right to refuse, stating that he felt sufficient vindication for his actions and, because the matter had become public record, he was satisfied he could work in the area without fear of reprisal.

Another example of the right to refuse helping to pave the way to workplace improvements was a mill lockout incident. A couple of boilermakers had been working for several days on relining and replacing the lip of an ore bin. In order to facilitate the job, it had been decided to leave the ore bin full and use its contents as a platform from which to work – a good option because it negated the need to build scaffolding had the bin been emptied.

In order to ensure that no ore could be drawn from the bin below, the pan feeder, a conveyor at the bottom of the bin, was locked out and isolated to prevent operation. When the workers returned the following day, they discovered the bin had been emptied over the course of the night shift.

How was that possible? They had the lockout keys in their possession. They quickly discovered that their lock had been cut off and discarded and that the pan feeder had been used to empty the bin of its contents of ore.

Again, the right to refuse was used because the lockout procedure, which was arguably one of the company's most important rules, had been violated and compromised, leaving a new sense of vulnerability to all who relied on it for protection.

The mines inspector was again called in to resolve the issue. The mill had a limited number of employees on the night shift, which was further reduced by those who didn't have any motivation for emptying the ore bin in the first place.

The culprit was asked to own up to his misguided action but held fast. Everyone on shift was interviewed by the mines inspector but his investigation drew a blank as to who the person was who had cut off the lock.

The ore in the bin had been needed to keep the mill operating so there was a clear understanding of why the bin had been emptied. How it was done was also easy to determine because bolt cutters were available in the area. Because there was no confession and no witnesses to the crime, it remains unsolved to this day.

What the incident did do, however, was place much more accountability on all employees locking equipment out. Shift bosses and area supervisors were required to document the release of and return of equipment to operating status and date, time, and signatures were all recorded in a formal logbook. Strict procedures were put in place should a supervisor be required to remove an employee's lockout protection in the event that he had left the property and was unavailable.

No similar incidents of this nature occurred and confidence in the lockout procedure was re-established.

Ongoing Hazard Recognition

Recognition and control of a hazard is one of the cornerstones of health and safety, yet it is sometimes only after an incident has occurred that the hazard becomes obvious. New York's 9/11 disaster is a good example. Prior to 9/11, it could not be envisaged that five people could get on a passenger airplane, take control of it, and deliberately fly it into a building, let alone have this happen with multiple planes at the same time with different targets.

One of the immediate outcomes from that terrible event, besides increased airport security, was the securement of the cockpit of planes to prevent access to the pilot during flight. Every passenger plane's cockpit quickly became a fortress with steel doors locked from inside. This was a legitimate solution to an unauthorized person ever again getting into the cockpit without permission of the pilot.

Who would have anticipated that several years later, the same door would prevent a co-pilot, who had left the cockpit to use the washroom, from re-entering the flight deck, which meant he was unable to prevent the pilot from flying the plane deliberately into the side of a mountain, killing everyone on board.

Back in the mining world, a water pump in a pumphouse at the end of a dock on one of the nearby lakes had to be changed. It was quite a challenging job. A mobile crane could not get close enough to the pumphouse to remove the pump. The pumphouse had also been built around the pump, making the task of removing the pump even harder. A decision was made to use a helicopter.

A crew of carpenters were assigned to prepare the pumphouse roof for removal. Lifting slings were then attached to the roof and the helicopter came along and removed it, placing it off to the side. Everything seemed to be going according to plan.

The next part of the job was to disconnect all the pump's water lines and drive motor. Then lifting slings were placed around the pump in preparation for plucking it out of there.

As the helicopter hovered into position, the down draft from its blades created enough force within the confines of the four upright walls of the pumphouse to blow them apart. One member of the carpenter crew, who was standing close to one wall as it let go, ended up being catapulted into the lake.

Freezing cold water, heavy boots, and a carpenter's toolbelt fully equipped for every eventuality except a surprise swim in eight feet of water, meant he was going down fast! He was a tall man, but not that tall... Fortunately, he survived the ordeal to laugh about it with his crew later.

The incident resulted in the development of a policy for anyone working in, on, or around water. It included such things as availability of rescue rings, floatation devices and life jackets, none of which had been considered before.

In another incident, an employee was cutting the grass on one of the company's elevated lawns. He was using a ride-on mower and inadvertently drove it off a four-foot wall. He ended up lying on the adjacent roadway with a couple of cracked ribs and the mower on top of him.

The incident happened over a weekend and the very first phone call we received on the Monday morning was from our CEO. After expressing his concern for the injured employee, he wanted answers to some of the following questions:

- Do we have written procedures in place for grass cutting and using this type of equipment?
- What are the training requirements for this type of work, and has it been documented?
- Was the employee wearing a seatbelt at the time of the incident?

When you get a phone call like that from a CEO, if you don't have anything in place, you invariably do by the end of the day. Having had no exposure to ride-on mowers myself, it was interesting to learn that they don't come with seatbelts. Instead, there is a pressure switch under the driver's seat so as soon as his bottom leaves the seat, the rotating blade on the mower stops turning.

The answers to the other questions the CEO had posed were that grass-cutting procedures were developed by day's end for all HBMS properties. They covered PPE requirements, inspection of the cutting area for debris and suitability of equipment, and no ride-on mowers to be used on terraced lawns.

Also included but not all inclusive was equipment refueling, the need for insect repellent/bug netting, potential for heat exhaustion, adequate water supply to prevent dehydration, working alone, and more. The manufacture of the ride-on mower also had a useful training video on the equipment, which was to be used in the future.

A couple of electricians were checking out an overhead crane using a manlift. The crane they were working on had been locked out to prevent any unanticipated movement. They were then alongside the bridge 30 feet in the air in the confines of the manlift when along comes the safety representative for the area. He immediately warns them that they had not locked out the second overhead crane that operates in the same bay on the same rail track as the crane they were working on.

The safety rep's concern was that the other crane could potentially be operated and strike the manlift they were working from. He believed the second crane should also have been locked out. Thus, started a very interesting discussion on who was responsible for the safety of the two electricians.

"Somebody should have told them to lock the other crane out," said the safety rep.

"Who is the someone that should have told them?" asked their supervisor.

What about the supervisor of the area in which they were working… the one who issued them the lockout approval for the crane they were working on?

Perhaps, but did the electricians have no responsibility themselves? Are they not trained to recognize the hazards of the job and take care of them? After all, they had done the same job many times.

"Am I to remind my crew each and every time I assign them work to not forget to lockout the other crane in the bay?" the supervisor went on.

What was the hazard, and was there a real danger of somebody getting seriously hurt? Risk is proportional to how somebody perceives it, and their tolerance for it. Everyone has a different level of risk that they are prepared to accept. Some people would never engage in risky activities, mountain climbing, surfing, skate boarding, parachuting, etc. Others may have an even lower risk tolerance, their perception of danger being tempered by the activities they are prepared to engage in, like walking, jogging, playing cards, darts, curling, etc.

We have all stood at a pedestrian walkway waiting for the lights to change before we start across the street when somebody comes along and risks it by taking off a few seconds early.

The interesting thing about the crane story is that when the electricians came to set up the manlift and prepare to do the job, the other crane was not in use and was parked at the far end of the bay, almost the length of a football field away. Had that crane been operating close to their crane, it would have been a no-brainer to have locked it out because the hazard of an impact with it would have been more easily anticipated.

Were sufficient controls already in place without having to lock the other crane out in the first place? What were the chances of the anti-collision device that automatically prevented the two canes from striking each other failing when they were within 20 feet, or of the operator of the second crane failing to see the men in the lift?

Was the safety rep being overly cautious or was he 100 percent right in voicing his concerns.

When I worked in the steelworks, a crane maintenance crew had removed the top of the main drive gearbox and a rigger was standing with his feet inside the gearbox while he wrapped a sling around the first motion shaft to remove it.

Another crane operating in the same bay nudged the crane the crew was on and the rigger's feet were mashed by the gears that turned due to the motion of the crane. The rigger survived the incident but had to have both feet amputated. The safety control in place at the time consisted of bunting (flagging strung across the bay) to warn the other crane operator that the second crane was down for maintenance.

However, flagging does not stop a 40-ton crane in motion. Rail stops do! After this unfortunate incident, steel rail stops were bolted onto the overhead crane track ahead of a crane down for maintenance when there was more than one crane sharing the same track.

It wasn't that the possibility of cranes contacting each other had never been envisaged, or that the subsequent potential for injury had never been considered. The control that was used to mitigate the hazard just proved to be totally inadequate.

Similarly, red barrier tape only serves as a warning that an open hole exists. It doesn't prevent someone from falling into that hole. A much more physical barrier must exist, such as handrails or concrete blocks, etc.

A hazard can lay dormant for years and not cause a problem. For example, who would think that a shipping tag placed on the inside of a coil of steel rather than on the outside could cause a fatality?

Given the unique circumstances, an employee tragically lost his life while reading the information on a shipping tag as two coils came together, crushing his skull. The recommended action from the fatality investigation was that all shipping tags be placed on the outside, not the inside, of coils of steel.

Yet another fatality in the steelworks was that of a young operator siting on a handrail while on a moving overhead crane. As the crane moved down the bay, one of the building's support beams became a pinch point between the employee, the building, and the handrail and he was crushed as it passed by.

A government inspector was checking the maintenance elevator used inside Flin Flon's 825-foot smokestack. His arm was resting on the handrail of the two-person open elevator as it was travelling upwards toward the top of the stack. Suddenly, his arm was grabbed between the handrail of the elevator and the inside wall of the stack. He quickly pulled it away from the pinch point before the elevator had time to travel any further up the stack.

Had the inspector not reacted as quickly as he did, his arm would have been ripped from his shoulder. The pinch point did not exist at the bottom of the stack when he first got into the elevator and rested his arm on the handrail; there was a lot of clearance then. However, the stack is tapered and narrows toward the top.

This demonstrates the importance of ongoing hazard recognition because some hazards have a nasty habit of creeping up on you, as one did when a shift boss walked up to an underground piece of mining equipment to check on the equipment operator, who appeared to be asleep at the controls.

As he disturbed the operator, the operator inadvertently slumped back onto one of the equipment's control levers, which caused the machine to articulate, causing a pinch point exactly where the shift boss was standing.

The machine held the shift Boss in its grasp until another employee was able to climb onto it and move the controls back to their original position. Unfortunately, the shift boss had already sustained horrendous injuries. He was lucky to survive the incident but consequently was left severely disabled for life.

Some hazards are very easy to identify but hard to control. Everyone watching a blacksmith's air hammer striking its anvil with such force that it could straighten out a steel bar in a microsecond would instinctively know not to place their hands anywhere close to the impact zone.

Yet an employee had part of his hand mashed when it briefly entered the business end of the hammer to sweep aside some debris that had built up on the anvil.

How do you protect someone from a pinch point that, by design, was meant to be a pinch point? How could such a situation exist? This incident speaks to several contributing factors, as most do.

The job of straightening punch bars (10-foot long steel bars) was a daily activity in the blacksmith work area. The bars came in by the bundle and 50-60 per day needed to be straightened so they could be put back into operation.

The task of straightening them took two men. One operated the controls that sent the hammer up and down to strike the anvil. The other person held onto the steel bar, positioning it between the hammer and anvil, turning it slightly each time it was stuck until it was straight.

Once satisfied with the result, the straightened bar would be set off to the side and another bent bar would be picked out of the bundle and the process repeated. Communication between the two workers performing this task was non-verbal. If the employee holding onto the bar had to say "hit it" each and every time he needed a blow to the steel, it would probably have driven both of them insane due to the number of strikes needed to each bar.

In addition, both men were required to wear double hearing protection due to the high level of impact noise generated by the activity. A method of communication had been developed between both of them on when a hammer blow was needed.

The two men were positioned in closed proximity to each other so a nod of the head would send the hammer crashing down on the anvil. Once the hammer control lever had been activated, there was no going back. It was like firing a gun; once you pull the trigger you cannot put the bullet back in the chamber.

So, when the employee holding the bar noticed debris build up on the anvil and decided to sweep it away with his gloved hand, the hammer operator took the slight nod of the head that he saw at the same time as a signal to send the hammer crashing toward its unintended target. The next split second will be remembered by both employees for the rest of their lives.

There were a few contributing factors to this accident, but lack of experience or training were not on the list. Both employees were skilled and had performed the task hundreds of times before.

What did make the list was the shear repetitiveness and monotony of the task, which led to some complacency as well. One of the controls used to reduce job fatigue with a high degree of repetitiveness is the work rotation. The interesting factor in this incident was how seniority came into play.

One of the findings in the investigation was that both men, although capable, never spelled each other off. They always did the same task, with the senior employee always working the hammer and the more junior guy always holding the steel bar. After all, the hammer man, when he had been the junior guy, had held the steel bars for years and now, through progression, he had the better, less physical task to perform.

Another one of the worst accidents that occurred in the surface operation, which, fortunately, did not result in a fatality, took place inside a dust atomizer chamber. It's like a steel tank or large hopper with one door for access.

An employee entered the chamber to check and break up any hard lumps of dross (zinc oxide) that may have accumulated in the chamber during processing. He stepped off a work platform onto a moving auger in the floor of the chamber.

An auger is a shaft with flights built into it that transfer material (dust) from one end of the chamber to the other, just like farm augers transfer grain into silos. They resemble an ice auger except they run horizontally. As they turn, the dust is caught in each flight and moves along the length of the auger.

The employee's foot and boot started their journey around the flight of the auger. If it continued to turn, the auger would have drawn not only his foot, but also his leg and, potentially, the rest of his body around the auger like a meat grinder.

Fortunately, his safety boot with its steel shank and toe caps offered enough resistance to trip the electrical breaker to the drive motor. The Motor Control Centres, rooms in which the electrical breakers are located, are accessed only by authorized personnel, such as electricians. The MCC room was particularly hot on that day due to ambient temperatures in the area. This was also a factor in the breaker tripping.

The employee was still in a precarious position. His foot was firmly lodged around the flight on the auger and had been crushed inside his safety boot. He was also alone. His screams for help managed to attract the attention of another employee who was passing the outside of the chamber.

Emergency paramedics were called and the task of trying to extract the employee's foot from around the auger began. Maintenance personnel attempted to turn the auger in the opposite direction by hand using a pipe wrench on the gear box drive shaft. That might have worked except for the fact that the employee's other foot also began to be drawn around the auger's flight. As one foot was coming out, the other was going in.

Over 20 minutes had passed and the employee was screaming to have both feet cut off, fearing that the auger might suddenly start up again and consume him entirely. The temperature inside the dust chamber at the time was well over 30C. Such chambers were never meant to be occupied during normal operation for any prolonged period of time.

Other considerations in the rescue attempt were to try cutting the auger from its housing, which would not have been an easy task because it was made of stainless steel and an air arc would have had to be set up rather than a mere cutting torch. That fact in itself would have created a lot of fumes and smoke inside the chamber, making the atmosphere even less tolerable.

The employee's foot was finally removed after his leather boot was carefully cut off and his foot was released from the auger's steel grasp. He had a few broken bones in one foot, but the injury paled in comparison to what it might have been.

Among other things, the subsequent investigation identified an obvious issue. Why wasn't the auger locked out to prevent movement? The company had strict rules and procedures for working in such situations. If the auger had been locked out the incident could not have happened. Why hadn't the employee locked it out? Did he not know? Was he new to the job? Had he been trained? All these questions were raised.

The facts spoke for themselves. Yes, he had been trained and was very experienced. He had done the job many times without an issue. He had not locked the equipment out because he believed he had turned it off at the control switch. He also believed it was not turning when he stepped onto it.

Poor lighting inside the dust chamber, the slow turning speed of the auger, and the fact it made hardly any noise at all reinforced his belief. The investigation concluded that his foot could not have travelled as far into the auger by just slipping around the flight; the auger had to have been turning.

Accident investigation and discipline do not go hand in hand. Never the two should meet, but there may well be a need for discipline when a rule violation takes place under certain circumstances, but that is the roll of Human Resources and involves a completely different review.

In any event, if you were to dig deeper into this incident, you would find that going into the atomizer chamber was routine and performed several times a week by different personnel.

Employees just don't decide that it might be a good idea to go inside to inspect and break up the hard lumps that sometimes accumulate. They are assigned the work by their supervisor. The supervisor is also required to release operating equipment in his area of authority by issuing and documenting locks and tags to ensure that equipment is properly isolated.

Documented evidence that the atomizer chamber auger was being isolated (locked out) on the same frequency as that of the work being done could not be produced. The area supervisor should have wondered how the work was being done without him having to issue the required isolation locks, tags and record keeping requirement through the lock logbook.

Task observations by supervisors on members of their crews are intended to confirm that critical tasks their employees perform are being done correctly. If the supervisor performed a task observation on employees performing the task of entering the chamber, he might well have identified that lockout procedures were not being followed as they should be. Employees relying on a control switch rather than an isolation switch could have been corrected. That's the Monday morning quarterback syndrome, or acknowledgment that hindsight is 20/20 vision.

When performing accident investigations, it's important to understand that their purpose is to gain a complete understanding of why the accident occurred so that preventive measures can be put into place. If the focus of attention during an investigation is only on the individual involved, system failures might be overlooked.

On the other hand, if you can identify and fix system failures that have contributed to an accident you are far more likely to achieve your goal of preventing a recurrence. If you only try to fix the individual involved, he or she may never have a similar accident, but others might.

A heavy equipment operator in an underground mine was driving up the ramp to surface not long after the start of his shift. The transmission on the equipment unexpectedly shifted gear causing a lurching motion, which, in turn, resulted in the operator being lifted from his seat and hitting his head on the roll over canopy of the equipment. He landed back in his seat with a heavy thud, suffering a jarred neck and bruised tailbone.

The subsequent investigation determined that the transmission oil in the equipment was very low, almost off the dip stick, which was the probable cause of the unexpected shift and lurching motion on the ramp. The investigators also determined that there had been no catastrophic failure that would cause the sudden loss of transmission fluid.

Equipment operators at the mine, as in most mines, are required to complete a pre-operation check of their equipment at the beginning of their shift, including a check of all fluid levels. Results are to be documented and turned into their supervisor. Investigators could find no evidence that the operator had carried out the pre-operation check at the beginning of the shift in which the injuries occurred.

It would have been very easy to reach the conclusion at that time, that had the operator performed the pre-op, the transmission fluid would have been found to be low and topped up. This, in turn, would have prevented the incident from happening. The investigation could have wrapped up citing the operator for failing to carry out a required inspection prior to operation of the equipment. Fortunately, the investigation continued.

The investigation team then looked at other mobile equipment that was operating in the mine. Were other required pre-operational checks getting done? No evidence was found to suggest any required documented checks were being carried by any equipment operators on any of the equipment.

What the investigation revealed was not that just one operator had not carried out a required pre-op but that there was a complete breakdown of a management system. If this was a finger pointing exercise, it would be easy to say the equipment operators should be disciplined for not doing an important part of their job and thereby, in some cases, putting multi-million-dollar equipment in jeopardy.

However, once completed, pre-operational inspection sheets go directly to the supervisor of every shift. The supervisor's roll is to review them, note any deficiencies reported by the operator and then issue work orders to the maintenance department to have the necessary repairs done.

You have to wonder why a supervisor who, as part of his responsibility, was supposed to review and take action on completed pre-operational equipment checks, would not be questioning why his in-basket lay empty every shift.

In another example, a supervisor had filed pre-operational forklift inspections and a forensic review of them revealed that one operator had noted on his daily pre-op on 26 consecutive shifts that the back-up alarm was not working. We must hand it to the operator for his persistence and patience. Many would have given up noting the concern way before 26 times.

It isn't just supervisors that put themselves in jeopardy when it comes to not demonstrating due diligence. Some workers also shirk their responsibilities by failing to live up to their obligations.

Signing a crane logbook to indicate that they have completed their maintenance check when they haven't been anywhere near the crane, is one example. Recording meter readings when the meters hadn't been visited is another.

One of the key attributes expected of a supervisor is that they know their crew members, their strengths and weaknesses. They are expected to intervene if any of their personnel are not performing to expectations or are not being their normal selves. One of the reasons supervisors are expected to be so vigilant is because it is required of them under Workplace Safety and Health regulations.

The overhead crane in a surface garage was ripped from its rails when an employee drove a forklift out of the building. The rear end of the forklift had been suspended by the crane and a sling was still attached to both. Two employees working in the garage at the time of the incident narrowly escaped serious injury as the crane dropped to the floor below.

Investigation interviews revealed that the employee driving the forklift had "gunned" it out of the shop, forgetting to remove the sling beforehand. There was enough momentum to dislodge the crane from its rail mounts.

Interviews also revealed that it was a normal day in the garage. The person involved often displayed his frustration by swearing, throwing wrenches, spinning wheels, etc. The result came when the general foreman, who was leading the investigation, summoned the employee involved and the union safety co-chairperson, who was also a union steward, to his office where he handed the employee a three-day suspension slip.

What went wrong with that investigation? The golden rule of investigations was broken. Never use an accident investigation meeting to determine if discipline is justified. That it not the purpose. The purpose of the investigation is to determine cause and make recommendations to prevent their recurrence.

Discipline of employees involved in accidents is a separate thing. Discipline requires a completely different approach. Personnel involved include HR, union officials, etc., and there is a different anticipated outcome. It may involve progressive discipline or some time off, but it may also determine if the employee involved needs some assistance in dealing with personal issues that may have been an underlying factor.

It is always a good idea at the start of every accident investigation meeting to reiterate its purpose. Introduce everyone at the meeting. Let everyone know that the purpose of the investigation is to have a clear understanding of what took place to reduced or eliminate the likelihood of it happening again. It is sometimes a little harder than it sounds. Especially if you have some strong personalities and emotions in the room.

An incident that involved a mobile crane operating too close to overhead power lines provides a good example of how a group of people can sit at the same table and have different reasons for being there.

Not only did everyone not know each other, half the people at the table believed they were there to review the incident to prevent it happening again while the other half believed a supervisor was about to be disciplined so they had shown up to prop up his defence.

Not only did the meeting go badly, it could also have easily been handled differently. With little effort, its purpose could have been properly communicated early on, and the participants properly introduced at the start of the meeting.

For that matter, another good idea when investigating accidents is to limit the number of people who are going to participate.

When an express warehouse delivery truck hit the side of a rail car being moved by a locomotive, there was no shortage of people wondering how such a collision could have taken place.

Due to the fact three different departments were involved, warehouse, surface and transportation, and the train and track crew, representatives of each were invited to attend the review meeting. In total, 18 people filed into the meeting room.

The truck driver, who was uninjured, was asked by the lead investigator to describe what happened immediately prior to hitting the rail car. Everyone in attendance went silent waiting in anticipation of his response.

"I blew the Stop sign," the driver said. "I wasn't paying close enough attention."

End of investigation? Well, not quite! It could have been but, fortunately, it was decided to form a small group to review the incident in more detail. The rail crossing itself was perhaps the worst one you could ever imagine. It was poorly marked, ran at an angle of 30 degrees to the track, and was not used by the truck driver on his regular run. He had been diverted the morning of the incident due to a road closure on his usual route.

A worthwhile list of recommendations was produced as a result of taking a more in-depth look. Lesson learned: Don't give up on an investigation when somebody just wants to take full responsibility. You might just miss something that needs to be addressed.

In another investigation, the event was recorded on video camera. Two ore truck drivers approaching from either side of a security gate stopped for a chat. Neither driver got out of his vehicle. They just lowered their windows.

One ore truck was clear of the gate but the other one, which was pulling a double trailer, was parked with the first trailer through the gate and the second on the other side of the gate. The gate rolled into position from one side of the road to the other. A camera recorded what happened next.

The gate closed after timing out. Its leading edge stopped between the two trailers being pulled by one of the ore trucks. Both drivers were unaware that the gate had closed and after their conversation had ended, the truck with the two trailers took off, ripping the gate and all its hardware with it.

Open and shut case? Again, not quite! Even though it was clear on the video what had taken place, the follow-up investigation revealed several relevant facts. The sliding gate had been purchased to restrict access to the mine site to authorized traffic only. It needed to be operational 24/7, year-round.

One of the issues the investigation revealed was that the gate was not "fit for the purpose," which means that for most of the time, the gate was not functioning due to mechanical or electrical issues. This was prevalent during the sub-zero temperatures of our Northern Canadian winter months. Other gate issues included batteries freezing up and ice and snow being contributing factors.

When carrying out investigations, issues such as engineering and purchasing decisions can play a significant role in the outcome of an event. Having to "re-engineer" something only means that it can be improved upon from its initial design or specifications. An automobile is a prime example, otherwise we would all still be driving around in black Ford Models Ts.

Not everyone sees and has the same perception of a hazard, especially if the task has been carried out successfully before without incident, like the smelter furnace wash down.

Anticipating hazards in the workplace and ensuring workers are fully aware of them sounds easy. It is the supervisor's duty to inform the worker of any hazards when assigning the work.

Knowledge is Power

It would be great to be able to tap somebody on the shoulder and tell them to take the rest of the day off because they were about to have an accident.

Health and safety departments haven't quite got it down to a science to that degree. Reality is more like a fortune teller's crystal ball. However, there are some accidents that we know are going to happen ahead of time. Slips and falls increase substantially in the early and late winter months – like snow and ice melting, thawing, and then refreezing just in time to catch the morning shift on the way to work or coming home from the night shift.

Minus 7 Celsius is the worst temperature for slips, which are most likely to occur in high traffic areas such as parking lots, entrances to buildings, and walkways. These areas also get the most attention when it comes to maintenance, snow removal and sanding. Yet, each year they manage to claim their victims. Again, with some amount of predictability, the severity factor comes into play. The older you are when you fall, the more likely you are to suffer a more disabling injury.

Toddlers just learning to walk almost seem to bounce with no consequences while a person in their 70s or 80s is looking at broken hips, etc.

Eye injuries are also predictable in nature due to the high volume of them occurring, and yet they are the most preventable of all injuries. Wearing safety glasses in the workplace has always been a general rule, just as it is expected that hard hats are to be worn. Yet the number of head injuries compared to eye injuries is disproportionate, especially considering your eyes are in your head. This is because eyes are much more vulnerable. Even a speck of dust can cause an issue.

All this would suggest that something is out of sync. Safety glasses do a pretty good job when it comes to small impacts. They do a lousy job when it comes to fine dust, liquids or chemicals, in part because they were never designed for those things. Yet we continue to focus on the fact that an employee dutifully wearing his safety glasses is following safety standards.

What the employer and employee should be focusing on is the appropriate eye protection for the work being done. Just like selecting the correct tool for a job, safety equipment is specific.

I lost track of the number of times I have seen people working at heights wearing a body harness and lanyard attached to enough rope that would allow them to hit the ground before it came into play. They were wearing all that fall-arrest equipment to appease the safety requirement, not to actually prevent personal injury. Wearing safety glasses in dusty areas or around chemicals amounts to the same thing.

So how can we prevent injuries if they are so predictable? I believe one way to start is by shifting attention from safety glasses to appropriate eye protection. If we provide a new employee with safety glasses on his first day on the job and only stress the importance of wearing them at all times, we have missed a golden opportunity. That opportunity is to also add chemical and dust goggles and perhaps a face shield to their arsenal of protective equipment, with the expectation that they will be chosen according to the need at the time. As the worker moves from task to task, he can use the best eye protection he has to fit the immediate need.

Theoretically, eye injuries could be eliminated completely. Wow! That looks like zero, at least for eye injuries! If it were only so simple...

Indeed, knowledge is power and education breeds knowledge.

The workplace hazardous information system was introduced at roughly the same time that I entered the safety field, almost 30 years ago. It revolutionized the workplace in as much as it started to educate workers on the dangers and consequences of chemicals and substances they were being exposed to as they worked.

This knowledge added a new dynamic in many ways. For the first time, workers were being given very specific training on every-day products they were using (in some cases, incorrectly) that could have long lasting health effects, including cancer.

Clay, oil-absorbent pellets, for example, had been used in the surface and underground operations of the mine for years. The absorbent came in 50-lb. paper sacks and we used tons of the stuff for soaking up oil spills in the main workshops and machine areas. It was brought in by the pallet load. The only information on the bags of pellets was the brand name, weight, address of the supplier, and details on how to re-order.

Workers sometimes transferred the pellets from bags to empty steel drums where scoops were placed so that when the product was needed, the scoops were filled, and the pellets thrown in abundance onto the offending oil spill. The pellets lay there on the ground doing their job of soaking up oil, sometimes for days. Eventually, when they became saturated, they were shoveled up and disposed of.

I remember a new shipment of absorbent pellets arriving shortly after the WHMIS regulations had kicked in. They were the same pellets we had used for years. The only difference was that the bag was stamped with a cautionary label warning the user that the product contained a silica dust that was cancer-causing. The label also advised that they be used with appropriate personal protective equipment, including a respirator.

The new knowledge that the users of the product had acquired through the mandatory WHMIS training caused them to be horrified at the thought that they had been using such an unsafe product in an unsafe manner for years and had inadvertently been exposed to a cancer-causing agent.

Hence, alternatives were investigated and, low and behold, a very similar product was found as a suitable replacement. The new product had no warning labels on the bag, so it was assumed to be safe. Great! No issues!

A large order was placed for this new, safer absorbent and the offending absorbent with the warning label was returned to the supplier. Everyone felt pretty good about how things had transpired. After all, one of the objectives of WHMIS was to increase employee awareness and find suitable, less harmful products to use in the workplace. If only issues could always be resolved so easily!

Soon after the old absorbent was returned to the supplier, however, we received a frantic call from the product's manufacturer. They felt aggrieved that because they had complied with the WHMIS regulations and correctly labeled their product and supplied the necessary Material Safety Data Sheets, they lost an important customer.

Upon investigation, we thought we had switched to a safer product only to find out that we had changed to one that was under scrutiny by regulators for failing to comply with the new regulations. In fact, the replacement oil absorbent contained higher levels of silica! The solution was to switch back to the oil absorbent that we were using originally and ensure that employees were using it as recommended and wearing the appropriate PPE.

It was an important lesson to learn. At the time, we had nearly 5,000 MSDS sheets on products that were in use at the mine. It seemed like just about anything and everything had become hazardous. One of the notable spinoffs from WHMIS was that it created a greater awareness of just how many chemicals were infiltrating the workplace and, in some cases, completely unnecessarily.

When inventories had to be taken, just the number of free samples alone that had been dropped off by well-meaning salesmen while visiting supervisors was unreal. All had to be accounted for and MSDS sheets obtained. It soon became apparent that past practices had to come to an end. No longer could sales reps bring in free samples without first supplying the corresponding MSDS forms for scrutiny. No longer could supervisors request a new product without justifying why they needed it and what product it was going to replace.

We were also very fortunate because the mine was a large enough enterprise to have industrial hygienists on staff. They had the expertise to review all the MSDS sheets and pinpoint the really nasty stuff – chemicals that would be problematic in use, storage and/or disposal – and not permit approvals to take place that would allow those products on site.

One of the exercises we went through in the early days was to inventory all the chemicals we had on site. You cannot control what you don't know about. One workplace inspection we went through was to determine what was being used by our carpenter crew. We went through all their tools, storage lockers, and bench draws and amassed a whole bunch of aerosol cans, sprays, adhesives, solvents, etc. We then purchased a proper non-flammable steel storage container and put all the bounty we had found into it.

The carpenter boss, who was "old school," looked at the new storage container filled to capacity and said, "All you guys have done is build yourselves a bomb."

The fire chief with me at the time replied, "At least we know where the bomb is."

One of the other spinoffs of WHMIS was to get rid of all the stuff we had no clue about, stuff that was decanted into unmarked containers and that had sat for so long nobody could remember what it was, or why it had been spared. Lots of times it was a mixture of waste oil or solvent, but with no ready means of identification, it was painstakingly disposed of.

Another WHMIS benefit was to reduce the types of products that all did the same thing. Examples included about six different varieties of penetrating oil, such as WD-40 and Liquid Wrench, which were similar in nature and used for the same purpose. Everyone had a favourite but by going to a single product, you only needed one MSDS and you could purchase the product at a premium discount because you were buying in bulk.

WHMIS was one of the cornerstones in the new safety era. It helped transform the workforce by having workers engage in their potential health risks, both short and long-term. They started to question scary stuff, like asbestos, PCBs, lead, cadmium, etc., most of which they had worked with for years.

Abatement programs started to be introduced targeting asbestos and PCBs, Lead substitutes were found where possible. Lead was eliminated in products such as paint and children's toys, new transformers were built that did not contain PCBs, and older transformers were drained, isolated, or decommissioned.

Improvements were also made to personal protective equipment, air-quality monitoring, biological monitoring, and employees' exposure to such things as noise. Health and safety committees became more engaged by monitoring the workplace for compliance to the WHMIS programs.

One of the down sides was that there was a lot of technical information on the MSDS sheets. This information was provided for professionals, such as industrial hygienists and doctors. But it became part of the training for the average worker and was confusing and often outside their level of understanding. Consequently, WHMIS training became somewhat boring for many. Years after its introduction, it seemed to have lost its initial influence on changing people's habits.

Seldom was a request made to review an MSDS by a worker who was about to use a product for the first time. Instead, most requests for the data sheets came in after an event or incident had occurred with the product, which was unfortunate because the main purpose of WHMIS was to be proactive, not reactive.

As with many new initiatives, they tend to lose momentum after a while. Labels that once caught the eye and generated concerns started to become mundane. A really good example was when cigarette packages started to display warning labels that their contents could be hazardous to your health. That may have stopped a few people from smoking, but after a while, those same labels were seen as not effective enough, so they were followed by images on the cigarette packages of diseased lungs and other "sick" organs.

Again, it may have had the desired shock effect and caused a few more people to consider quitting but it remains true that despite the warnings of cancer and the graphic pictures of lung and heart decease on packets, people still continue to smoke.

Hazardous products only become a danger to the user if the instructions and warnings are not heeded. It's possible for them to be used perfectly safely.

It has been my observation, and one that I am guilty of, that men are not very good at following or reading instructions on packages. They tend to put things together and refer to the instructions only if doing it on their own doesn't look right or they have pieces left over.

One accident that I was part of the investigation of involved a hazardous product. A spray solvent called Slap Shot had been used inside a dismantled crusher. The employee using it had sprayed it on the main bushing he was cleaning. After a few minutes, he switched on a small electric tool similar to a grinder. A spark from its motor was enough to cause the vapour inside the bushing to ignite.

There was a pop, which probably lasted only a microsecond, but sufficient energy and heat were released to burn off all the worker's facial hair. It also caused first degree burns to the skin on his face, which was not protected by the half-mask respirator and safety glasses he was wearing. It also burned off the paint on the respirator filters and melted the back of the neoprene gloves on the employee's hands.

The can of Slap Shot carried several warnings on the label, including being highly flammable, and to restrict its use to well-ventilated areas. The inside of the crusher bushing was a confined space and not well ventilated.

The employee was wearing flame retardant coveralls at the time so his injuries were superficial compared to what they might have been.

That was an example of how a product presents itself to be a hazard when not used as it was intended but the packaging warnings are ignored.

WHMIS training, along with other key health and safety training, has been handed off to computer-based training modules in many cases. They are okay for the generic content that employees need to know about regarding the key elements of WHMIS but, in many ways, they fail to address the specific needs of individual workplaces and the hazardous products that the employee will be using day to day.

As a footnote to trainers, if you or the employees you are training have entered the workforce in the last 30 years, they have not had the experience of a workplace that doesn't have workplace labels, MSDS, and training programs. Many people prior to the regulations taking effect paid a terrible price. Many had shortened retirements or a reduced quality of life due to the long-term health effects of working with hazardous products the nature of which they had not been made aware.

We owe it to them to train the workforce of today with vigor and enthusiasm so that the mistakes of the past are not repeated in the future. Employees and employers need to be reminded that it's not just another WHMIS training session. The information they are being given could ultimately save their life one day, or at least prolong it.

From on high...

When you identify potential hazards in the workplace, it's always a good idea to look up. Overhead hazards present a high risk of serious injury. A term often used in accident investigation, "Struck by or Stuck against" is meant to identify what caused an injury. Believe me, you don't want to be struck by a load being moved by a crane.

One of the primary reasons for using a crane to move a load in the first place is because it is usually large, or heavy, or both. Otherwise, it would be handled manually.

Hardhats are used to reduce injury severity. Unfortunately, some objects that fall to the ground are large enough and heavy enough that a hardhat becomes totally ineffective. When a crane block or bucket of a front-end loader comes crashing to the ground, a hardhat just doesn't cut it.

Fortunately, crane incidents are few and far between. They are serious enough to warrant the mines inspector, the involvement of a safety and health committee, and management representative being notified in a joint investigation.

One such incident involved an overhead crane at an underground crushing station. It had been worked on by an electrician. The work identified that the upper crane limit needed to be replaced but a new one was not readily available. The electrician had locked out the crane while he had done his initial inspections but had removed his personal lock once he had determined the repair could not be completed for a few days.

A short time later, the crane was put into operation by one of the workers in the area. The empty crane block, the business end of the crane that houses the crane hook and cable sheaves, was being raised to its park position after use. The block is usually parked just below the upper limit on a crane. The upper limit is often tested by easing the block slowly into the upper limit until the crane hoisting mechanism automatically stops.

What generally happens when a crane block passes through the upper limit and the limit doesn't activate, is that it carries on to the hoist drum where an immovable force meets an immovable object. The crane block cannot wrap itself around the hoist drum, so something has to give. Usually, the hoist cables break and the crane block and hook come crashing to the ground – several tons of steel fall 30-40 feet in a matter of seconds.

The crane operator in this case got a glancing blow from some of the falling material and received severe injuries but was extremely fortunate to survive.

The focus of the company lockout procedure had always been the protection of workers while they were performing work on or around equipment. The conclusion reached by the mines inspector as part of the investigation of this incident was that, "Equipment that is not fully serviceable should be protected from inadvertent start-up by being de-energized and locked out."

To allow equipment in a partially dismantled state not to be secured put workers in the area at unacceptable risk. A second lockout tag was introduced (Equipment Out of Service Lock and Tag). The new tag supplemented the personal lockout tag that was in place at the time and was to be used whenever equipment was being left unattended but was not fit for service.

Another incident that came inches away from a certain fatality involved the deliberate removal of a crane's upper limit. The reason that happened was to gain the extra few inches needed for a large convertor hood to be placed on a flatbed truck. The procedure had been carried out several times in the past. It was a critical lift and, again, was performed successfully.

After the convertor hood had been secured to the flatbed truck and the slings removed, the crane's upper limit was supposed to be reset. However, the electrician that had been called to defeat the limit, was not available to reset the limit because he had been called to another job.

The overhead crane was then used for another job by a different operator who sent it down the bay to its park position using the remote control. As mentioned, crane blocks are usually parked just below the upper limit. In this case, since the crane's upper limit had previously been defeated, the block went into the hoist drum, sheared the cables and went crashing to the ground beside an unsuspecting machinist who happened to be standing alongside his lathe.

To say that several tons of steel missed him by inches would be an understatement. In fact, the hoist block not only missed him, but landed on the only open space on the concrete floor that was large enough to accommodate it.

Another incident occurred when maintenance personnel were performing an inspection of the hoist gearbox on an overhead crane. It's a good example of how a safe job procedure is useful, particularly when the work is not done on a regular basis or the workers have not done it before.

Most work performed on equipment starts off the same way: de-energize and lock out. The crane was moved to its park position and the lockout procedure was followed. The crew started to get rigged in and do the work. The bolts in the hoist gearbox top cover were removed and the gearbox cover was lifted clear to enable the gears inside the box to be inspected for wear.

But as soon as the top of the gearbox was clear of the rest of the gearbox, the first motion shaft and gear popped upwards, no longer being kept in place by the gearbox top. The hoist block and cables went free falling to the ground below as the hoist drum spun freely, no longer restrained by the gear from the first motion shaft.

Fortunately, again, no injuries! The resulting investigation concluded that prior to locking out the crane, the lower hoist limit needed to be removed. The crane block could then be lowered completely until it rested on the ground below. With the crane block's weight off, the crane could be de-energized and locked out. The top of the gearbox could then be removed without any potential of the hoist block falling to the ground. It would have nowhere to go because it would already be safely in place.

The purpose of the lower hoist limit on an overhead crane prevents the hoist block from being lowered too close to the floor during normal operation. When changing crane cables and removing the top of an overhead crane hoist gearbox, it needs to be identified and removed. After the work has been performed, it is replaced as part of safe-work procedures prior to putting the crane back into service.

Cranes get a lot of attention. They are highly regulated and the controls in place are there for good reason. Consider the amount of effort and resources it takes to operate an overhead crane: daily pre-operating inspections by qualified crane operators prior to use; weekly, monthly and yearly inspections by licensed tradesmen; crane logbooks detailing operating use and maintenance history… just to name a few of the controls.

Then there is the training required to operate an overhead crane. At one time, the crane operator controlled the crane from the crane itself while sitting in the crane cab positioned just below the crane bridge. This is still true for some cranes today. That vantage point allowed the operator to see everything looking down from above the crane hook.

The operator relied on others at ground level, known as riggers, to hook up and disconnect the rigging of the load. The rigger was responsible for estimating the weight of the object being lifted, determine what size of lifting slings to use, and how they were to be attached. The crane operator and the rigger worked as a team once satisfied that the load was correctly hooked up to the crane.

Through hand signals, the rigger would guide the crane operator to raise, move and lower the load to wherever it was needed. The rigger and the operator required different skill sets. Both had received basic training and then honed their competency with experience. The more experience they gained, the more competent they became. Crane operators and mobile equipment operators require good hand/eye co-ordination and concentration.

One of the changes that I observed during my time in mine maintenance and safety was the use of remote controls to operate a greater number of overhead bridge cranes. They operate on rails close to the roof rafters inside a building and travel its length. A "bridge" that spans the width of the building carries the hoist and cross travel. The crane is able to pick up anything at any location in the building, provided it doesn't exceed its capacity.

Mobile cranes, as the name suggests, are mounted on chassis. They can travel to where they are needed but care must be taken around energized overhead power lines, and the ground they operate on must be capable of supporting them and their load.

No longer are some of the cranes operated from a crane cab. In many cases, they are being operated from ground level. The same person that rigged the load to be lifted, also moves it by remote control. This adds a new dynamic to the use of overhead cranes and reduces some of the risk of crane use.

Having the crane operated from ground level eliminated the use of hand signals and the possibility of a miscommunication. The crane operator on some lifts also takes on the role of rigger by being able to select the slings, hardware and attachment points. As a result, he became totally responsible for the lift.

One incident occurred many months after a new overhead crane had been installed in the main machine shop. It moved ever so slightly without anyone touching the remote controls. The operator reported the incident and the crane was locked out and underwent a complete inspection by electrical and mechanical tradesmen.

Nothing wrong could be found with either the crane or the remote-control box. After extensive testing, the crane was put back into service and performed without further issues… until a few weeks later when it moved again without the controls being touched.

This was a serious problem because many precision lifts were made with the crane and any unanticipated movement could cause injury to people in the vicinity. Again, an extensive check on the crane and controls could find nothing wrong.

The crane was put back into service and several months passed with flawless operation. They say three times a charm, which was certainly true in this case. Again, the crane moved without anyone touching it, but this time somebody observed something else happening at the same time.

The machine shop was a large area covering approximately the size of a football field. Two cranes ran on the same overhead rail track. They were used to move material and equipment around in the work areas below. The far end of the shop was the machinist section with lathes, milling machines, etc.

The middle section was where maintenance mechanics carried out repairs on pumps, gearboxes, and a host of other equipment used in the surface and mine operation. At the far end of the shop was the boilermaker/welding section.

On the third occasion that the crane malfunctioned, it was noted that the unanticipated movement had occurred over the boilermaker/welding section. The crane rails had been checked on prior occasions for any deviation that might have contributed to the unexplained movement and found to be okay.

The two previous incidents had also occurred over the boilermaker/welding area, although not in exactly the same location. The crane was then operated over the offending section of the machine shop in every conceivable configuration and, again, no issues.

A good accident/incident investigation always keeps asking the same questions. Why? So why does a perfectly mechanically and electrically sound crane malfunction once in a while? Why does it only malfunction in one area of the shop? Why does it malfunction only once in a while? Why not all the time? Why was the second crane that operated in the same area not having the same issues?

If you keep asking why, you invariably find some answers. The answers kept coming. The difference between the areas of the shop was the work activities that were taking place below. One activity was unique to that area, although it was not continuously happening. That activity was also taking place throughout the whole of that area.

What was the difference in the operation of the two cranes? They were both controlled by remote control. Answer the riddle and the mystery is solved. We finally saw the light and the penny dropped!

The crane was moved into position over a workstation in the boilermaker/welding area. Its remote control was set off to the side so nobody could touch it. A welder was asked to start electric welding in various areas of the boiler shop. Nothing happened… until he struck an arc with his welding rod directly below the infrared sensor mounted on the crane some 30 feet above him.

Much to the delight of the multitude of onlookers who had come to witness the event. the crane moved. The puzzle had finally been solved! The difference between the two cranes' remote controls was that the older crane was radio controlled and the newer one used infrared technology. Once the new crane had been fitted with a radio controlled remote, the issue was finally put to rest.

However, having resolved an issue, a very good process in determining success is to ask one last question. Have we mitigated one hazard only to create another? The use of radio signals to operate remote controlled equipment can pose a risk because if a signal is sent to one piece of equipment and operates another, that could have tragic consequences, but it has been managed and regulated in underground operations for many years.

Also, the use of radio signals around explosives can pose a risk. As more and more pieces of equipment in surface operations of the mine became remote controlled, that, too, needed to be managed.

Technological Changes

A similar incident that was never resolved occurred when a remote-controlled electric locomotive moved unexpectedly. Someone who was standing next to it had their cell phone ring at the same time as the locomotive moved. The obvious thought was that the phone had triggered the unanticipated movement.

However, the movement could never be duplicated no matter how many times the cell phone was tried so it was put down to coincidence in the end. The technical people believed it was not possible for a cell phone to have caused the movement.

When you look back over the years to the changes in technology that have influenced safety, the cell phone must be high up on the list. Consider that in Ontario alone, they have become the number one cause of traffic fatalities, overtaking drinking and driving.

However, cell phones have also saved countless lives by putting the ability to call emergency services into everyone's hands, thus reducing the time it takes to find a telephone and get help from minutes to seconds.

But managing cell phone use in the workplace is a challenge. People at every level within an organization have become dependent on instant communication gratification. Text messaging has replaced the verbal grapevine that used to exist. Don't get me wrong, the old grapevine was fast, but text messaging is a whole new ball game. Add social media to the mix and you have the potential for huge problems.

Let's take a serious accident or even somebody taken seriously ill at work as an example. It only takes one inappropriate text message to be relayed and family members of those affected could instantly find out that their loved one may not be coming home from work as expected – not a good way to find something like that out.

There is never a good way of communicating to family members about an event of such a serious nature, but people deserve and should expect the dignity of being given tragic news face to face by a company representative or an RCMP officer.

So how do we manage cell phone use in the workplace? One of the recommendations I make to supervisors is not to wait for a serious incident to happen before trying to address the problem. Talk to your employees and make it clear that in the event of an accident, serious illness or incident in their work area, the use of cell phones, text messages, or photos to dissipate information into the community is unacceptable and could subject them to discharge.

Some of the horrific images that exist in serious accidents are, unfortunately, inescapably captured in the minds of onlookers forever. They don't need to be captured on digital imagery and posted for random curiosity seekers forever!

At the same time, the use of digital photography in accident investigations is invaluable. To demonstrate how much has changed over the last 30 years. I used to have to wait for a roll of film containing accident investigation pictures to be developed. It could take two to three days depending on what day of the week it was when I dropped it off. When taking the pictures, I was always mindful of how many I could take and how many were left on the roll.

Then came one-hour photo development and our thirst to get at the facts asap got even stronger. One-hour was soon eclipsed by the Kodak instamatic for a few short years until, finally, the age of digital photography rolled in. Government inspectors investigating accidents had to carry two cameras for a while because the new technology could either not be trusted or the pictures could be subject to editing.

Today we can click away to our heart's content and take hundreds of photographs for later scrutiny from every angle of an accident scene. The photos have become invaluable, not only in the investigation process itself, but also in teaching and explaining to others what had taken place. The saying that a picture is worth 1000 words is certainly true in such a case.

A word of caution, though. A digital camera cannot capture temperature, noise, or how fast things are moving, but it can automatically compensate for poor lighting conditions. However, all the environmental conditions need to be captured accurately, not as "adjusted," and then noted in subsequent reports.

Workers' Compensation

nother significant change that has taken place in
health and safety over the past 30 years is the way
injured workers are accommodated. This came
about partly as a result of spiraling workers' compensation
costs being levied against employers.

A certain philosophy existed that employers paid for
workers benefits in Workers' Compensation Benefit levies,
rather like insurance premiums. Should an employee be
injured on the job, the worker received uninterrupted
financial support to cover their lost wages until they were
considered fully fit to resume their normal duties. Any
interference from the employer by offering to bring back
the worker early might put the payments being received
from the WCB at risk.

As a result, many workers injured on the job received
compensation for years, some never returned, staying on
compensation until they retired. As employers' WCB
premiums continued to rise each year, it became obvious
that the status quo could not be sustained. Something had
to change, and quickly.

Workers Compensation premium assessments that
employers pay are based on a number of things, including

the type of industry and number of claims by individual companies within that industry.

Accident frequency rates are based on an industrial standard of exposure. For example, how many injuries occur in 200,000 hours of work? The lower the number, the better. The common goal of most companies would be zero. However, having zero injuries is a stretch for large companies that employee hundreds of workers.

A more realistic goal might be to look for a decline in accidents/injuries year over year, so safety awards are used to encourage employees to work more safely. Safety awards at the mine were discontinued after several years because employees were perceived to be discouraged from reporting accidents if that would put their crew's group safety award at risk. Another problem with depending on numbers of injuries to determine if your safety systems are working is that they can distort reality.

One of the concerns raised when "modified work" was introduced to bring injured workers back into the workforce before fully recovering from injuries was that it looked like an attempt by companies to show their accident severity frequency rates were improving.

Severity rates were also based on a formula like that of accident frequency rates: number of days lost as a result of an injury for every 200,000 hours of work. They were used to reflect the severity of an injury. Obviously, a minor injury might only take a few days to recover from, as opposed to something like a broken leg.

Another concern that some employers voiced was that employees on modified work abused the system and stayed in the program longer than they needed to rather than go back to their pre-injury job.

In my experience, the modified work program provided many benefits to most employees who participated in it. In any benefit program, you will always get some who will abuse it or take unfair advantage, but they were definitely in the minority.

I remember viewing a video tape that had been sent anonymously to our safety office by a disgruntled employee. The tape showed a person off-loading turf from the back of a truck by hand. The video also showed the person carrying the turf and then laying it in position to make a lawn. The video lasted a couple of hours and was fast forwarded a few times until the work was complete.

The question asked was what was wrong in the video. I thought the lifting technique was pretty good. The person worked hard and could have used a wheelbarrow to reduce some of the carrying.

The correct answer was that the person in the video had not been to work for the previous six months due to a back injury and was claiming workers' compensation. This fact had infuriated the person who had filmed the employee to such an extent that he wanted to bring it to the attention of the company.

The video had been made without the knowledge and permission of the employee who was featured in it, so it was inadmissible. However, the employee was notified that it had been brought to the company's attention that he appeared to have fully recovered from his injury. He returned to full duty a few days later.

The modified work program also served a dual purpose when it came to injuries and long-term illness. Not only was it made available to employees injured on the job but was also provided to employees injured off the job.

You need a certain amount of empathy with these programs to believe in them. Good health, like water, is too often taken for granted. You only miss it when it is taken away from you.

The benefits provided by the modified work program far outweighed the very few employees who chose to abuse it. Many employees attached an unjustified stigma to the "Mod Shop" as it was called. The purpose of the Mod Shop was to provide meaningful work while employees were recovering from injury without jeopardizing their recovery.

It was also seen as being more beneficial to have employees return to a work environment and the social network that exists in a workplace than to isolate him or her at home.

Case management for injured employees helped drive down WCB assessment fees. Most WCB claims are settled, usually in the employee's favour and in a timely manner. The WCB requires three pieces of collaborating information in order to make a settlement, which are very basic. In most cases declined by the board, it is because one of those pieces of information is not being provided when required.

The employer has a requirement to notify the WCB within five days if an employee sustains an injury at work that requires treatment by a medical practitioner. If they don't, they risk fines and loss of credibility.

The injured worker has a responsibility to notify the employer and the WCB of any injury that incurred on the job and required medical treatment. A patient who receives treatment from a medical practitioner is required to notify the practitioner when they believe their condition is work related. The medical practitioner issues a medical report on the patient to the WCB that supports findings consistent with a workplace injury, or not.

Sounds pretty simple! It's all about communication, so what could possibly go wrong.

I would say the No. 1 reason for claims being denied or taking a long time to resolve is communication. When communication between the four interested parties (employee, employer, medical practitioner and WCB) become blurred, misunderstood or, in some cases, are non-existent, then frustration and anger sometimes set in.

Some examples of communication breakdown are when an employee is reluctant to report an injury to his supervisor in the first place. Back injuries are notorious for late reporting, partly because when they occur the injured worker believes the pain is temporary and that he will recover by the next shift. But, in many cases, the injury gets worse and after a restless break, the worker notifies his supervisor that he won't be able to make it in for his next shift.

The injured worker's supervisor has a responsibility to document and report all injuries to any employee. If the employee did not mention the back injury when it occurred on the previous shift, it is already a late report because the date of injury does not match the reporting date. This is a flag to both the employer and the WCB, adding the possibility that the injury might have occurred off the job. It does not mean that every late injury report is fraudulent. In fact, the majority are legitimate. The lateness just adds to the mix.

When the injured worker fails to get medical attention right away, still believing the injury will get better with rest, the matter is further complicated.

Then there is the paperwork required for medical practitioners to complete to support a compensation claim. If they are not told specifically during their initial consultation with the injured patient that the injury was work related, they might assume that it occurred at home.

The best advice I can give to anyone injured at work is to report it to your supervisor as soon as it occurs, seek medical attention, and make sure the medical provider knows that it is work-related. Report the injury to the WCB, which can be done by phone. Then co-operate with the injury investigation, which your employer will want to complete in order to prevent a similar occurrence.

If your employer has alternate duties that can be offered to you during your recovery period, which will not have a negative impact on your recovery, accept them.

My advice to supervisors is to encourage the people that work for you to report injuries to you as soon as possible. Don't let it be a negative experience. Document the injury and the circumstances that caused it. If it is serious and a health and safety committee exists, notify the committee and have it involved in any subsequent investigation.

Injury Prevention

Remember, somebody got hurt on your beat and you want to understand why so that it doesn't happen to anyone else.

Some larger companies have purchased computer programs to help document and manage their accident reporting, Intelex being one example. These software programs sift through the information given and produce reports to senior management on a wide variety of issues. Such software can be useful in identifying trends, causes and system failures. Older supervisors tend to have issues with learning new computer skills, preferring the old method of filling out an accident form because its more user friendly and personal.

One of five ways to reduce workplace hazard exposure is to engineer that exposure away. Other methods are to eliminate the hazard altogether, which is by far the best choice; substitute the hazard for a less harmful one, such as using a less harmful chemical cleaner that can do the same job; apply administrative controls, such as rules and procedures; and increase use of personal protective equipment. Of these five methods, the latter one is the least desirable because it means the hazard still exists. PPE just creates a barrier to prevent contact.

Engineers have a responsibility to design tools, workplaces, and equipment to standards created over many years of lessons learned.

I attended a conference many years ago and took in a lecture by a world-renowned German ergonomist. At the beginning of his talk, he asked his audience to briefly look up at the ceiling in the conference hall and then back down again every time he tapped his hand on the table.

Meanwhile, he continued with his discussion on the role of ergonomics in the automobile industry, tapping the table every minute or so. His audience dutifully complied with his request, looking up and back down every time he tapped. As time went on some of his audience started to become increasingly aware that their neck muscles were starting to ache.

The speaker then proceeded to tell the story of the axle assembly plant where he had been asked to troubleshoot. One of the tasks that a worker had to perform was to fill truck axles with oil as they passed along the production line in front of him. The oil was dispensed from a gun with a trigger and nozzle that fitted into the axle's filler hole. The worker would then look at the oil meter mounted overhead until the right amount of oil had been dispensed.

Workers performing this task had a higher than average absenteeism rate, some complained of headaches and muscle spasms. The task seemed simple enough, but the problem was that it was being performed every couple of minutes each time a new axle passed by.

The speaker provided a very easy solution to the problem. He had a small light fitted onto the oil-dispensing gun so that when the required amount of oil had been dispensed, the light would come on and the worker would release the trigger and wait for the next axle. This eliminated the need for the worker to look up every couple of minutes, providing him with a much more comfortable work environment.

A similar situation occurred during the arc welding process many years ago. Welders would routinely flip up their welding helmets to insert a new welding rod or inspect their work. Many welders suffered constant neck and back issues.

Then came "speed glass" in the welding helmet, which would instantly darken as soon as a welding arc was struck. This reduced the number of times the welder nodded his head to begin the welding process.

Another innovation that improved the human dynamics of welding was the increased use of wire feed, eliminating the need to continually replace welding rods every few minutes. Wire feed also fully automated some welding applications.

One of the most repetitive of tasks before it was automated a few years ago was the stripping of zinc by hand from electroplated sheets. The "strippers," as they were called, numbered 50-60. They worked in a building called a cellhouse. The whole process resembled what the inside of an old car battery might look like and was about half the size of a soccer field. It contained rows of sheets of aluminum, suspended in a solution of acid and zinc. Over a 24-hour period, the zinc in the solution would attach itself to the aluminum sheets creating an anode. The anodes were then lifted out of the tanks, usually five at a time, with the use of a small crane on a monorail above.

The strippers would move to the end of the row and use a stripping knife in a downward motion to peel the zinc from the anode on both sides. Once the zinc was removed, the anode sheets were returned to their places in the rows.

It was heavy, manual, repetitive work and the conditions in the cellhouse, particularly in the summertime with the high temperatures, were hard to endure.

As an incentive, the strippers were allowed to start earlier in the morning when it was a little cooler. They worked hard, many relentlessly, not even taking the time for a coffee break or to chat with a fellow worker. Their goal was to get their allotted rows done and get the hell out of there!

To protect them from the fumes, they wore cloth masks held to their faces with a copper wire cage. Those conditions were sometimes hard to imagine, but once they had completed their work they could to go home. Their reward was a chance to earn tonnage bonus and a full shift's pay. Many an experienced stripper could be seen heading for the showers as early as 9 or 10 a.m. if they had had good rows and the zinc had not been too difficult to peel off.

One stripper stood out amongst all the rest. He took his time, worked diligently, always completed his rows and left after eight hours of work. He was the union representative for the area and believed that his coworkers were putting themselves in jeopardy by proving to management that more rows could be added to their daily regimen if they continued to finish three or four hours ahead of the end of their normal work day. He didn't just talk the talk, as they say, he walked the walk! A good trait to have when you are looked upon as a leader.

As a footnote. The cellhouse floor partially collapsed into the basement in 1989. Some of the main timbers supporting the tanks let go and the rows of zinc fell like dominoes. If the collapse had happened during the stripping process in the morning when the workers were there, the results would have been catastrophic.

As it was, the number of workplace injuries generated in the cellhouse became intolerable. Years later it was replaced with a modern automated version that resulted in the loss of all the stripping jobs. If ever there was a case for replacing a worker with an automated system that had to be it. Nobody should be expected to earn a living doing that type of work.

However, it also stands as a testament to the men who, for years, kept the zinc flowing out of the company so they could make a reasonable living for themselves and their families. Even burly, hard rock miners temporarily transferred into the cellhouse during a slowdown had a hard time coping with the conditions and the physical demands of the old cellhouse.

Repetitive injuries take their toll in many workplaces and sometimes just a small change can make a tremendous difference.

When credit and debit cards were first accepted at retail stores and supermarkets, the cashier was usually the person who swiped them through the debit machine. As more and more cashiers experienced the effects of aching wrists that sometimes led to Carpal Tunnel Syndrome, a solution was developed that still holds today. It's far better for the individual customer to swipe or insert his credit or debit card once or twice a day as opposed to the cashier swiping a card for every customer who makes a transaction.

More recently we have the introduction of the "tap" to more quickly and easily withdraw your funds from your account.

In another example of using ergonomic principals to make life easier with small changes to daily routines, a delivery person dropped off his packages of small parts, filters, bearings, etc. The packages were usually easy to handle, never particularly heavy and most would weigh less than 30 lbs.

On one occasion, a package or two were dropped off at a supervisor's office and set on the floor wherever space existed. Several supervisors received these packages in their offices at various locations throughout the plant. By designating a small table that could accommodate the packages as the drop-off point, the delivery person no longer had to bend to put them on the floor and the supervisor, in turn, no longer had to stoop down to retrieve them. This also eliminated a potential tripping hazard.

You may want to try this if you don't already. When you bring your groceries into your home from the store, instead of placing shopping bags or boxes on the floor, set them on the countertop or kitchen table before you start emptying them and putting stuff away. You will probably find it a lot easier on your back.

Workplace injuries are not just confined to the shop floor and production areas. The office worker also has potential hazards with which to deal. Injuries may not be as obvious but, nevertheless, they can cause severe problems over time. With the introduction of computers, workstations changed dramatically. Seating, lighting, glare from monitors, keyboards, even the air quality in office areas now needs to be considered.

One size does not fit all when workers are spending up to six hours a day or more at their desks. If working conditions are not given close consideration, injuries, such as eye strain, headaches, back and neck issues, Carpal Tunnel Syndrome, etc., can occur.

In recent years, a lot of effort has gone into recognizing these issues exist. Improvements to conditions that contribute to them, such as lighting improvements, adjustable workstations, improved seating and standing positions have been made.

Mental Anguish

Work Shouldn't Hurt would not be complete without a section on the mental anguish that is caused in some work environments. Mental anguish can be as significant as a physical injury, yet often goes unrecognized.

Changes to legislation have helped to recognize and deal with such issues as harassment, bullying, and intimidation, which go on at every level in many companies and organizations. They often come to the surface only when an extreme case results in someone getting discharged or, sadly, taking their own life or the life of another. It takes on many forms and is sometimes very subtle.

Yet, it has been my experience that seldom, if ever, does a discussion take place that considers the mental wellbeing of an employee at the time of an accident or near miss. It's just something that doesn't get talked about, mainly because of the comfort level of everyone involved.

One such incident investigation I was involved in was particularly troubling. The employee was well trained and experienced, had done the task many times before, and yet, on this occasion, had narrowly missed getting seriously injured.

In this case, the employee, who was young and had two small children, recognized that his mind had not been on the work that he was doing. In fact, during the investigation interview, he voluntarily stated that his wife had left home the previous evening, leaving him to find temporary babysitters while he was at work. He hadn't been able to sleep and was worried sick about how he and the children were going to cope.

As a result of making his supervisor aware of his difficulties, he was temporary re-assigned, given flexible hours and accommodated until he was able to resolve his personal difficulties. People at the Employee Family Assistance Program, with the resources to guide him through this difficult period, were made available to him. It is a good initiative for companies who invest and support employee and family assistance programs. They can provide invaluable counselling services when needed.

Everyone comes to work at some point or other with a certain amount of mental distraction and stress. It might be as a result of a sick child, an ailing parent, a failing relationship, or financial woes – just a few of the things any and all workers deal with. Often, these mental distractions are short lived; the sick child recovers, the failing relationship improves, but all take their toll.

High levels of stress in the workplace also occur when things don't go as planned: production targets aren't met, equipment failures occur, etc.

All this mental anguish manifesting itself in a person puts them in a vulnerable position that can lead to increased absenteeism, accidents, or HR involvement.

Heavy industry used to be a man's world, but more and more females are entering the trade groups to become mechanics, electricians, machinists, boilermaker welders, etc. There are no limits in their choice of skills. They are also taking up key positions within the mine and operations and seen as better equipment operators than their male counterparts. When a piece of mine mobile equipment can come in at over a million dollars, you need someone at the controls that can operate it with a little tender loving care.

When it comes to wage parity, there are no issues. Groups such as Women in Mining and Women of Steel have been formed not only in Canada but also overseas.

Back in the day, a supervisor had to be tough and show no sign of weakness, otherwise his crew would take advantage and walk all over him, or so it was believed.

Not anymore! A supervisor must be a coach, mentor, or counsellor, and needs to be successful in all his roles. Over the years, I have worked for some good and, occasionally, poor supervisors. I have also experienced some who abused their position of authority and took every opportunity to threaten and intimidate. Fortunately, it has also been my experience that these people eventually contribute to their own demise. Many because they had never nurtured loyalty and respect from their subordinates.

A key component of being a successful manager or supervisor is loyalty and respect. When poor supervisors eventually fall from grace within an organization, company, or department, there is usually a unified sense of relief that reverberates and uplifts the general workforce and, in some cases, even others in the management group.

It is not only the occasional poor supervisor, manager or executive that falls through the cracks and abuses their power or position. It can occur at every level within an organization, even worker on worker.

Robotics, Drugs, Alcohol, and Harassment

A friend of mine told me that at a time in her life when she felt most vulnerable, her full-time union representative tried to take advantage of her. She worked in a bakery from 3 a.m. until 10 a.m. It was a part-time position and she was trying to raise three small children after her husband had left her. She desperately wanted a full-time position because it would enable her to access the benefits package that came with a full-time job.

Her full-time union rep would often come into the bakery when she was on shift to check in on his members. He would, however, ignore the rest of his flock and make a beeline to the back of the store to single out my friend, who was young and attractive. She was totally not interested in his attention and just wanted to go to work, do her job, and get paid.

She eventually got the full-time position by default, working six consecutive weeks of more than 32 hours a week. Under the union contract, that automatically qualified her for the full-time position.

The union rep then intensified his quest for her attention. She was terrified when he came into the bakery because he would immediately go to her work area where she was mostly by herself and intimidate her by getting right in her face and saying such things as, "You owe me.

When are we going to get together? When are you going to pay me back?

Of course, his inference was that without his help, she would still be working part-time. It was a terrible predicament for her. She felt she had nowhere to turn. Her coworkers would help when they could by warning her if he came into the store, and by trying to distract his attention to give her a chance to hide until he eventually left.

These incidents happened almost 40 years ago but she still trembled when she told me about them. I can't imagine how she endured so much stress and tension at work every day just because she wanted to provide for her family.

With the advent of the Me-too Movement, and workplace harassment policies and regulations in place, situations like that should never be repeated. These predators, who still exist in all areas of life, need to be recognized for what they are. They need to be called out and removed from positions of power.

The introduction of robotics into the workplace has certainly made life easier for some, particularly where repetitive work is concerned. However, robots can present their own hazards. Keeping them apart from the regular workforce can also present challenges.

A certain number of serious injuries occur each year throughout all types of industries as a result of drugs, alcohol and other stimulants. In that vein, one of the biggest challenges that companies are faced with today is the legalization of "pot. How do we ensure that it doesn't become a contributing factor in work-related injuries? It would be very naive to think that it hasn't been a factor in the past.

As with alcohol, many highway fatalities name it as a major cause. The major difference in the past has been that when a significant highway accident occurred, testing for alcohol was automatic, which has been important because it either confirmed or eliminated it as a possible cause.

Similar testing must take place in the workplace whenever a serious event occurs for the same reason. We owe it to everyone concerned to properly identify the true cause of all serious injuries. Some companies are now moving in that direction; all need to follow-suit.

Companies are now required to have policies in place to deal with harassment in the workplace. This is a good thing, but an important piece is missing, which is how each case is handled. The general workforce and government agencies are kept in the dark in this regard.

I am not suggesting for a minute that we publicize each event. Confidentiality should always prevail, of course. However, how many cases of harassment are taking place within an organization each year: one or two, 10 or 20, or more? Are the numbers going up or down?

Just like companies with high accident rates, companies that have high numbers of workers reporting harassment need to be singled out. As with the Me-To Movement, change takes place when public awareness increases.

The Smelter

The smelter was one of the least desirable workplaces in surface operations, old and dirty and almost unbearably hot in the summer. Winter conditions were no better with temperatures that could reach −40C being drawn into the large open building.

Most of the work areas required the use of half-mask respirators as the minimum mandatory respiratory protection. The need for them was dictated by the presence of So2, cadmium, lead, silica dust and other harmful airborne contaminates.

Pressure leach eliminated the need for the old fuming plant that still stood as a testament to days gone by, and to the company's inability to secure demolition funds because of depressed metal markets.

The fuming plant was not the only major piece of plant that was rendered redundant with the existence of the start-up zinc pressure leach system, which was the first in the world using two-stage autoclaves. The dryers, two large cylindrical drums with brick furnaces and the zinc roasters also lay silent.

Unfortunately, not only were these buildings expensive to demolish but most also contained encapsulated asbestos.

Main support services such as steam, air and hydro, which still supported the remaining operation, ran through the redundant buildings. These services would have to be re-routed for any demolition to even begin, which would also escalate the cost.

The smelter was made up of four main areas: feed prep and roasters; the reverb furnace; the converter aisle, nicknamed converter pit; and anode casting. Tragedies had occurred in all four areas over the years, the reverb furnace and the converter aisle being the most recent to suffer fatalities… until that fateful night! Both areas process and move hot metal.

The converter aisle building housed the front end of the reverb furnace. It was approximately twice the area of a football field and housed three huge steel, brick-lined drums called convertors. Molten metal was tapped from the reverb furnace into large ladles poured into the convertor drums as part of the refining process, sand and air were then added in the converter.

At any given time two out of the three converters wherein use 24 hours a day, seven days a week, the third one being down for maintenance. Two large, 50-ton overhead cranes moved the ladles and sand pots around in the building.

The convertors rotated and rolled in and out from underneath giant convertor hoods that helped capture the fugitive emissions. Two large doors at each end of the building allowed access for the delivery of material and equipment. The north door of the building was one of the coldest areas to be in the dead of winter.

No "green space" existed between any of the smelter buildings. In fact, they blocked most daylight from each other. A smelter employee could work in one of the four areas for a lifetime without knowing anything about or doing work in the remaining three areas, unless he was recruited for shutdown duties. Smelter shutdowns were legendary, requiring a total team effort of skills and pure muscle.

In earlier years, the shutdowns were scheduled on an annual basis, which ensured experience and learning opportunities. In more recent years, shutdowns edged up to a three-year cycle. Logbooks were started to detail the sequence of events and problems encountered during shutdowns to stand against fading memories and ensure mistakes did not get repeated. At the same time, employees with a lot of shutdown experience were reaching retirement or taking pension windows.

Experience that was being gained at the entry level was also being lost when employees became eligible through seniority to move into the mine department. Wage bonuses paid to underground employees did not make such a move a difficult decision for most workers.

The smelter shutdown in 2000 was unique in four major ways. First of all, it was taking place in the early part of August, which had never been done before. Previous shutdowns had all taken place in the early spring or late fall when outside ambient temperatures provided relief from the hot, dirty, physically demanding work required to demolish and rebuild the reverb furnace, originally built in 1930.

The furnace got its name from the heat from the oil (12,000 litres a day) burners (two of four) at the front of the furnace reverberating over the bath of molten metal and slag contained within its refractory brick walls. The size of the furnace is slightly larger than a public swimming pool at 31 by nine metres, and four meters high. It had three levels: the top level or calcine floor, then the feed floor, and then the main floor.

One of the main safety concerns leading into the shutdown was risk of heat stress to employees. Training had been extensive in that regard, both in recognizing and preventing it.

In addition to the time of year that the shutdown was to take place, the smelter spill gas project, a $25-million initiative that was set to improve conditions and reduce airborne emissions throughout the surface operation and surrounding area, needed to be tied in and commissioned. That project would eliminate the need for a smelter bag house, by far one of the worst places to work in any smelter operation. It had been the method of reducing heavy metals going up the smokestack but would be made redundant with the spill gas project.

Other work scheduled during the shutdown period, which was slated to last about 14 days, was also a concern. The copper roaster dependency on coal was being eliminated with the use of propane, which would see an end to the coal plant.

The copper precipitator that collected the solids from the smoke prior to entering the stack was also receiving much needed attention.

With so many men involved with all the tie-ins and project work taking place during the narrow window of opportunity, workers were like ants in a new colony, which became the third major factor in the shutdown of all shutdowns!

The final major difference in the 2000 shutdown was the previously mentioned deployment of new methods and equipment to reduce the physical stress on the workforce. A skidder, a large cable drum machine with a grab bucket used in the mining department, was the traditional method of removing brick from inside the furnace floor. The machine was mounted on a flat rail car and operated by a single operator from the front of the furnace.

Problems encountered with this equipment in the past consisted of cable damage and snags, equipment breakdown, setup time, and lack of experience by the operator because the equipment was usually mothballed from one shutdown to the next.

The proposed new method of brick removal would eliminate the skidder by having a D7 cat operate within the furnace itself and push the brick out. Head room inside the furnace was tight so the safety committee had gained approval from the Mines Branch to remove the rollover protection from the D7.

The other obvious concern with the use of the D7 was the temperature inside the slowly cooling furnace in which it would be operating. The assurance that the equipment could be operated at such temperatures was reinforced by the equipment's traditional use in forest fire situations.

As an additional precaution, the use of two D7s would allow the equipment and operators periodic breaks away from the harsh environment of the furnace.

Two remote controlled hydraulic Brokk machines were also to be used. These machines would eliminate most of the jackhammer work traditionally done by labourers. One of the machines would play a significant role in the severity of injuries suffered by its operator.

When people share the same harsh environment that a smelter provides, a certain bond develops between them. You either tolerate the place or you hate it. Many people have spent a lifetime working in smelters and have enjoyed their experiences, mostly because of how people interact with one another. The Flin Flon smelter was legendary in this regard.

The bosses of old knew how to manage their men. They were firm but fare. Incidents, equipment breakdowns, and production problems occurred daily, but their resolve and innovation matched the challenges that personnel were confronted with.

Another thing about shutdowns was "the other shift syndrome." It was felt between crews that they should always do or achieve more than their cross shift. Apparently, this is common in most industrial settings and certainly has been the case in this writer's experience.

When guys get together to work on a project that involves tear down and rebuild of anything, a certain macho pride kicks in. There is an underlying momentum that drives each crew to complete its work better, and faster. The second that a shutdown begins, the clock starts to tick. How long it will take before a fire is back in the furnace is on everyone's mind. How long before the long hours of working through days off will end and everything is back to normal?

An interesting thing about human nature is that supervisors who are held accountable for part of a project are overwhelmingly focused on ensuring they are not the reason for the project's failure or time overrun, so much so that they fail to support the rest of the project if doing so puts any risk on their own assignment.

A Gantt chart or a critical-path chart is often used to timeline and sequence events of a complex shutdown. They enable the work to proceed in logical steps. They have a start date and projected finish date, with all dates in between indicating whether the work is on schedule, ahead or behind schedule.

One of the first shutdown activities is to empty the furnace of all molten metal and slag. The last activity is to light the burners. Who would have thought that as the shutdown began, it would be months, not days, before the burners would start to roar again and the furnace temperature would start to rise?

One of the issues that came to light immediately after the explosion was that one of the main man doors leading down from the furnace to the outside of the building had been padlocked from the outside. This is somewhat of a reflection of the lack of discipline and lack of compliance to some rules that were poorly structured and in effect at the time.

A CAT 988 loader, the biggest in Hudbay's fleet, was used to clear an area in front of the furnace at ground level. The loader is large and only just fit through the huge double doorway into the north end of the convertor pit, which housed the west end of the reverb furnace. The man door in question was at the foot of the stairs leading to the second floor and giving access to the reverb furnace.

Concerns had been raised in the past that as you exited the building from the man door, you were within only a couple of feet of being crushed under the wheels of the 988 loader if it was entering or exiting the north end of the convertor pit. In order to control this obvious hazard in the past, red danger ribbon had been used to deny access through the man door whenever the loader was operating in the area.

However, the ribbon was often ignored by employees, who simply lifted it and passed under. Because they faced no consequences, the use of ribbon to restrict areas was not very effective, hence the reason for the padlock on the man door. The intention was good; its application was a mistake.

Another doorway in and out of the mechanics' shop was less than 20 feet away on the same side of the building. Better controls were in place there to prevent pedestrian traffic from stepping out of the building into rail and heavy equipment traffic, including a flashing red light and audible alarm inside the building to warn of impending danger.

Safety is not just about the identification of hazards in the workplace, but also about ensuring that controls selected to mitigate the hazard are effective, and at the same time, do not create another hazard or dangerous situation.

Barrier tape is useful and is used to warn or restrict access in countless applications in various situations. Its effectiveness can only be measured in terms of personnel being compliant with its use. If barrier tape is not removed promptly when the hazard no longer exists, or if the reason for placing it in the first place is not obvious, or has not been communicated, employees will disregard it and a more effective control needs to be put in place.

The locked door did not have the same impact as in the 1991 example to follow, but it did exacerbate an already very bad situation and could have made matters much worse. Valuable time and effort were expended as workers scrambled for an alternative means of escape.

In 1991, a chicken processing plant caught fire in North Carolina. Twenty-five workers died in the fire as a result of being trapped behind locked or blocked doors; another 40 were injured. Lessons learned from the past must be used to create a safer future.

In Flin Flon, the last fatality prior to the smelter explosion had occurred five years earlier. That had been the longest period between fatalities in the company's history. There has not been a work-related fatality in the 17 years since the explosion, but that is not to say the battle to create a harm-free workplace has been won.

We could so easily have had fatalities many times over those years. Sometimes the outcome was a question of sheer luck or twist of fate, a matter of inches, or seconds making the difference between life and death. It is those incidents that did not receive the same attention and resolve as the smelter explosion did that make it all the more important to revisit and communicate the important lessons learned from them. I have included many of them in the second part of this book under "Work Shouldn't Hurt" along with other examples I have experienced in my 49 years in the work force.

Lessons can be learned every day. They can apply to everyone who goes to work. It doesn't matter if you are a CEO, manager, supervisor or worker, everyone is an important cog in the wheel.

The smelter explosion became a watershed moment for the company, company employees, family members and all residents of Flin Flon. Like 9/11, nothing would ever be the same again.

The Explosion

The reverb furnace explosion occurred at approximately 1:40 a.m. Aug 8, 2000. I was outside of the building when it occurred, having left the furnace barely 10 minutes before. I had been with two of the bricklayers who were removing tile and had left with them when they completed their task. I had been asked to check on a forklift that had been left with its forks in the raised position and had found an operator to lower them.

As I started to walk back toward the furnace building, I heard a large popping sound followed by a series of bangs that must have lasted more than a minute. At the same time, I saw the brick shed building's west wall, which we were almost adjacent to, shaking violently. I, and another person, ran to the mechanics shop and up the stairs to get into the reverb area to find out what was going on.

Dust and heat filled the air. I could barely make anything out, but we had flashlights with us and somehow managed to find our way to one of the lunchrooms. A small group of men was there, including a supervisor. He said the furnace had exploded and that six people were still unaccounted for.

The supervisor and I then left the lunchroom and began a systematic search of the furnace using our flashlights as our only means of being able to see anything. Most of the lighting in the area had been blown away by the explosion and dust continued to fill the air.

As we searched each level of the furnace, starting from the calcine down, feeling our way along the catwalks desperately hoping to find someone, our hopes began to fade. After we finished our search, we headed back to the lunchroom where we were greeted with the news over the radio that all six employees had been accounted for and were in the smelter warehouse.

Nothing could have prepared me for what I was about to witness as I went to the warehouse. When the radio call had come in to say that the six missing personnel had been accounted for, there was no indication of how grave the situation was. I headed right over as best as I could through the maze of debris and darkness and reached the outside of the building less than half an hour since I had previously stood there, but it now resembled a battlefield scene from the movies. Men were everywhere, some in small groups consoling each other, others just standing or sitting in disbelief.

Four of the six who had been missing were in water-gel blankets from head to toe to help cover their wounds. Their workmates were comforting them. Just then, the first ambulance arrived. I went out and met with the attendant and asked how many they could take.

"Two lying down… four if they are able to sit," she replied.

Due to the severe nature of their injuries, it was decided to take all four at the same time. The men somehow managed to shuffle themselves out to the ambulance with the help and encouragement of their workmates. They were seated in the back and the ambulance took off to the Flin Flon Hospital. I cannot say enough about the bravery of those injured men, and how well their workmates cared for them as they awaited treatment.

As other ambulances started to arrive, personnel with lesser injuries waited patiently for their turn, making sure those whose injures where greater got priority. When everyone who needed it got medical attention, the superintendent arrived from the hospital and called everyone that was left to a meeting in the main meeting room. He said everyone was being allowed to go home and if they had any questions, concerns, or anything they could contribute, to leave their name with me and they would be contacted in due course. The shutdown was cancelled pending an investigation. Everyone left the room. Nobody approached me with anything that needed to be followed up on.

A short time later, we received a call that there was a strong smell of burning wood. The fire chief and I went looking for the cause. We found smoke coming from an annex building by the smelter change house, probably the result of the explosion. We stretched out a fire hose and I started spraying into the building from the tin roof while the chief put in a call for the rest of the fire crew to respond. I was a member of the company fire department at that time.

As the day crew started to arrive on site, I was asked to attend a debriefing with them before I left for home. I was totally exhausted! My wife had been frantic with worry having heard that there had been an incident but unaware of any of the circumstances. I couldn't and didn't want to talk about the events that had taken place. I was devastated by what had happened. It was one of those things that you know will stay with you for the rest of your life. You will never get over it. It was the worst night of my life.

Post-traumatic stress counsellors were brought in to deal with the aftermath. The whole workforce and their families were in shock and grief. In such a small, close-knit community, everyone knew someone who was deeply affected.

Steven Ewing died from his injuries after a valiant fight for his life. An inquest was finally held into his death almost eight years later, after being delayed by legal battles. Lawyers for the company successfully fought to gain access to transcripts of interviews done by the inquiry council with employees at the plant. The inquiry had not been willing to give up transcripts, but an appeals judge sided with the company in withholding them.

The workplace health and safety investigation concluded the explosion was likely caused by the water sprayed on the furnace coming in contact with hot, molten metal.

I was interviewed by the joint health and safety committee, as was everyone on shift that night. The Manitoba Health and Safety Workplace Division held a separate investigation, as did the RCMP. I was not interviewed by either as part of their investigations.

One other smelter shutdown had taken place in 2006. No water was used to wash down the furnace prior to demolition and rebuild. A company specializing in furnace shutdown and rebuild had been brought in to manage the project, which was successfully completed without major incident.

In early June, 2010, the smelting operation was permanently shut down because it could no longer meet the constant changes to government environmental emission standards.

A total of 14 workers, 12 employed by HBMS and two by contractors, sustained physical injuries in the 2000 smelter explosion, which included severe burns, lung damage, eye injuries and dust inhalation requiring those men to be sent to Flin Flon General hospital. After receiving first aid on site, seven employees were hospitalized while seven others were treated and released.

One of the Brokk machines brought in to reduce physical labour by reducing the need for workers using jack hammers contributed to the disaster. It was controlled from a control box strapped to the operator's waist with an imbecile cord running from the control box to the machine. At the time of the explosion, the operator was tethered to the machine and had to unstrap the control box in order to escape. This took additional time and contributed to his distress. He was one of the four who suffered the most extensive injuries.

As a result of the subsequent investigation by Workplace Safety and Health, changes to regulations were enacted to ensure that operators could no longer be attached to remote control equipment in such a way. A break away method was introduced and mandated so that an operator need only walk away from the equipment he was operating to become detached.

In addition to the physical injuries sustained by those employees, there were many others on shift that night who were also affected. As well, those who were not on shift, along with family members of the injured, suffered psychological trauma that continues to affect their daily lives. A total of 43 of those individuals filed Workers Compensation Board claims for stress and 28 individuals lost time from work.

Hudson Bay Mining pleaded guilty to one count under the Workplace Safety and Health Regulations, in part recognizing that that action would spare family members and the community the ordeal of going through what would have been a long, drawn-out trial. They were ordered to pay the maximum fine under law, which, at the time, was $150,000, plus a victim surcharge.

Although health and safety programs had existed at Hudson Bay Mining for some time prior to the explosion, they were not seen as adequate in properly identifying and controlling the hazard that existed that night.

It made little difference that shutdowns had successfully been completed in the past using water to wash down the furnace support beams and other areas to reduce worker exposure to dust during the subsequent demolition. In fact, that history only reinforced the general feeling at the time that the wash-down was not as critical a job as it turned out to be. The need to train, quantify the task, monitor and measure the outcome of using water around the furnace had been an oversight that became blatantly obvious after the incident.

One of the outcomes of the smelter explosion was that safety systems at Hudson Bay Mining were re-evaluated and the old DNV Loss Control Program that had been in place for many years was shelved. In its place, the company put all of its resources into becoming certified to ISO 18001 standards, an internationally recognized business management system.

To put this into perspective, and I do not wish to give credit to any one individual or system, in the first 60 years of operation, HBMS averaged 1.5 fatalities a year. A total of 90 employees had lost their lives. This number, or any number for that matter, is deplorable.

The most recent statistics from the Workers Compensation Board of Canada for the year 2017 indicate that 951 workplace fatalities took place in Canada. This was an increase of 46 over the previous year. Among those deaths were 23 young workers 15-24. Everyone would agree these numbers are unacceptable.

We must always be open to rethinking the way we do things. Change must be constant. To go to work each day without getting hurt has to be an expectation we all have.

Some employees seem to have the ability to suck the oxygen out of a meeting room with their negativity. Their focus is on the problems they see. Very seldom do they offer suggestions or solutions. "I see that it's broken; you fix it! That's your job; that's why they pay you the big bucks."

Unfortunately, life doesn't work like that. Safety is everyone's responsibility. It's far better to be part of the solution than part of the problem. Safety is often a matter of opinion and opinions can differ greatly.

Staggering Losses

April 28 marks the day set aside each year to remember all workers who have lost their lives or who have suffered life changing injuries across Canada. The Hudson Bay Mining Fatality List was handed out at the main gate in Flin Flon several years ago to serve as a reminder to all.

The number of employees who went to work one day never to return home to their loved ones at the end of their shift is staggering:

1929
Henry Krucko: Overcome by gas and crushed between the cage and timbers.
Harold Flage: A miss-hole exploded.
Jacob Holt: Caught between a belt and pulley.
Knut Eie: A scaffold collapsed; he was caught in a flow of concrete.
August Szulta: Drowned after his canoe capsized.

1930
Burnjulf Steinnarsen: Fell 180 feet down a shaft.

J. McKenzie: Fell from beams to the floor in a building under construction.

Yanne Ratianen: Fell 620 feet after being struck by a counter balance.

William Hasson: Fell 120 feet down a raise.

John Sierkerski: Fell through the open doors of a shaft.

Matti Ekola: Fell 600 feet down a shaft.

1931

Mike Jakubowski: Suffocated in a rush of sand and gravel.

John Mackay: Crushed while jacking up a machine.

Anker Edoll: Fell 35 feet from one level to another.

Anbroz Wresilovich: Fell 260 feet down a stope.

1932

Mike Gornik: Fell into a stope.

Clarency Muters: Crushed between a car and the wall.

Fred Halak: Crushed by a car.

1933

John Bloom: Caught in a belt.

Paul Rusnak: Fell from a skip.

Mike Lehty: Killed by a rock fall.

Xavier Suterlittle: Killed by a rock fall.

John Martel: Killed by a rock fall.

1934

George Porvaznick: Fell 80 feet after his safety belt broke.

Anton Korpan: Killed by an explosion in an open pit mine.

1935

Martin Gornoc: Fell 280 feet down a shaft.

1936
Peter Peloch: Fell down a stope.
Eli Potkonjak: Fell down a raise.
Eric Sanderson: Died of head injuries.

1937
Marko Obradovich: Buried in a muck pile.
Steve Benedik: Killed in a blasting accident.

1938
Poto Zlatkus: Struck by a scraper.

1939
Ronald Ward: Crushed by a fall.
Paul Huszti: Fell down a shaft.

1940
David Martin: Fell from a roof.
Frederick Lipton: Caught by a conveyor belt and crushed.

1941
J Machuga: Jammed against a wall by derailed car.
J.F. Divall: Killed by arsenic gas.
W. Soltys: Killed by a muck slide
R. Musgrove: Fell 185 feet down a raise.
Philip Lauterer: Crushed by a train.

1942
Kjarton Halldorson: Fell 24 feet after a plank broke.

1947
Alexander Bonwick: Electrocuted while cleaning a transformer.
H.K. Modden: Crushed after two trains collided.

Carl Redahi: Buried in a muck slide.

1948

Edwin Franks: Died of head injuries, rail stuck in shaft came through the cage.
William Greening: Crushed by loose.
John Miller: Gassed during blasting.

1950

John Finnson: Buried in muck when a chute collapsed.

1951

Matthew Gibney: Fell 30 feet down a raise.
James Birnie: Was electrocuted and fell from a ladder.

1952

Edwin Saxbee: Electrocuted
Dennis Corney: Died of carbon monoxide poisoning.
Ivan Armstrong: Died of carbon monoxide poisoning.
Franklin Vawter: Crushed by a mucking machine.

1954

Douglas Ketchen: Struck on the head by a scaling bar.
James McQuaid: Electrocuted.

1955

Paul Krassilowsky: Hit by Marion shovel.
J. Szabo: Underground.

1956

G. Simpson: Struck by hung up muck.
A.J. Peterson: Struck by falling sheave block in converter pit.
W.Bell: Underground death.

Victor Ostrowsky: Underground death.

1957
Paul Shalansky: Struck by hung up muck.

1958
John Filip: Buried by sand.

1959
Edward Martin: Buried by muck.

1961
Carl Esbenson: Died after fall (Chisel Lake).

1962
Mike Smoliga: Overtaken by the third car in a cross cut, which rolled him.
C. Ulinder: Caught between 15 ton car and timbered chute.

1963
Gilbert Sandgren: Bar he was using pinned his head against a plugged chute (stall)
R. MacKenzie: Underground.

1966
George Gamble: Underground (Osborne Lake).
Robert Renas: Crushed by a slushing machine (Stall Lake).
Hope Forster: Shock as a result of a broken leg.
Edgar Leslie: Head injuries while installing a 4-inch water line.

1967
Elmer Anderson: Fell from ladder (Chisel Lake).

1968
George Clark: Crushed by locomotive.

1969
Donald Hoffman: Crushed by loose (Chisel Lake).
Van Costello: Fell 35 feet from a catwalk.
Malcolm Stewart: Runaway train in Smelter.

1971
Tim Leslie: Fell 144 feet down a shaft (Anderson Lake).
William Scott: Injuries received in a blast (Chisel Lake).
Ronald Short: Injuries received in a blast Chisel Lake).

1973
Andrew Makich: Crushed by ore car (Stall Lake).
Patrick Quinn: Fell down a wine (Stall Lake).
Russell Spence: Fell from Anode Casting Roof (TMCC).

1974
Frank Stadnyk: Fell down raise (Aurora Drilling).

1975
Brian Good: Crushed by feed that fell on him in a dryer.
Gordon Watt: Electrocution (flash burns).
Peter Gauthier: Fell down shaft (Patrick Harrison at Dickstone Mine).
Alaine Drolet: Fell down shaft (Patrick Harrison at Dickstone Mine).
John Shea: Buried in run of muck (McIntyre at Osborne Mine).

1976
Jerome Schermann: Fell 50-69 feet down No. 2 Pocket dump.
William Watson: Fell 215 feet down a shaft.

1977

Douglas Fenwick: Struck by loaded skip.

William Denby: Asphyxia at top of backfill cone (Stall Lake).

Thomas Campbell: Asphyxia at top of backfill cone (Stall Lake).

Edward Holden: Crushed by loose (Stall Lake).

Lindsey Sjuberg: Crushed by loose (Stall Lake).

Louis Boudes: Grinding Wheel disintegrated (PD&B Blasting) (Stall Lake).

1978

Robert Cameron: Crushed by Loose (Stall Lake).

1979

Paul Macer: Buried by hydraulic fill and water.

1980

Lorne McMillan: Fell 285 feet into an ore pass.

Duane Rupp: Standing on a skip that fell 90 feet (Stall Lake).

John Sinclair: Hit by loose (Aurora Quarrying at Spruce Point).

1982

Vernon Cochrane: Fell 40 feet (Aurora Quarrying at Rod Min).

1985

James Young: Fell down a raise (Spruce Point).

Glen Wood: Fell 1925 feet (Spruce Point).

Kenneth Burrows: Crushed by loose (Stall Lake).

George Jesso: Crushed between moving ladle and concrete wall.

1986

Lawrence Evachewski: Crushed by loose (Chisel Lake).

John MacKinnon: Buried by waste muck.

Ghislain Labrecque: Fell 110 feet (Aurora Quarrying (Namew Lake).

1987

Vernon Chilson: Asphyxia and possible electrocution.

1989

Alvin Moore: Electrocution (Aurora Quarrying (Namew Lake).

1991

Gordon Ferchoff: Crushed by loose.

Reginald Keating: Crushed by loose.

1992

George Gehon: Crushed between a low bed and work bench (Snow Lake Garage).

Clarence Funk: Hit by fly rock during a blast.

1993

Cliff Mitchell: Crushed by a scooptram (McIsaac Drilling at Callinan).

1994

Kevin Puetz: Fell down 55 feet stop while operating a scooptram (Ruttan).

Robert Jordan: Fell down 120 feet stope while operating a scooptram.

1995

Walter Walsh: Crushed by loose (Ruttan).

1996

Richard Beasley: Burned in overhead crane.

Eric Smedegaard: Smelter burns.

2000

Steve Ewing: Smelter furnace explosion.

This fatality list demonstrates the tremendous sacrifice employees have made over the history of Hudson Bay Mining and Smelting. Many workplace safety and health regulations have been implemented as a direct result of the lessons learned.

The list does not cover the tremendous number of accidents that did not result in death but did inflict life-changing injuries. It also goes without saying that fatalities and serious injuries always have a tremendous impact on family members and community.

Every name on the list represents a son, brother, uncle, husband or father, and many represent every single one of those relationships, which left wives without husbands, children without dads.

In the early years, it was clear by the numbers alone that loss of life was inevitable in the mining industry. Not anymore! In today's world, averaging 4-5 fatalities a year would get you shut down.

Regulations, new mining methods, increased awareness, improved procedures, and personal protective equipment have all contributed to reducing the likelihood of a fatality. Yet we can never be satisfied that we have done everything we could to prevent the next one. On the afternoon of June 10, 2010, the last copper charge was removed from the smelter's converters. A couple of final puffs of smoke and an era had come to an end. No more smoke, no more fire!

Many variables exist when people are put to work. Safety is easy to define, being mostly about common sense. However, when you throw in the human element, it becomes a lot more complex.

Biography of Brian Humphreys

Over 49 years of experience in steelmaking and mining as a tradesman and as a safety professional, both in the United Kingdom and Canada, has given Brian Humphreys a unique perspective from which to write about the Flin Flon mine disaster of 2000.

Born in Chester, England, in 1951, Brian spent most of his early years in Buckley Flintshire, North Wales. He attended Elfed County High School until he started working as an apprentice fitter at 16 years of age with the British Steel Corporation, Shotton Steelworks, in Deeside, North Wales. He continued his education during those four years of apprenticeship by attending Kelsterton College of Technology.

As the main provider of work in the area, the steelworks were fully integrated at that time, making strip steel from Iron ore and employing more than 13,000 workers. Brian's father, sister, brother and grandfather, as well as uncles and other family members were all employed there.

In 1979, the steel industry in Britain underwent a radical change under the Thatcher Government. Older steelmaking plants were phased out in favour of modern steelmaking facilities. Shotton Steelworks could not survive the cuts – almost 10,000 steelworkers were made redundant overnight, decimating the whole of Deeside and surrounding area.

Brian took the opportunity to look farther afield and responded to an advertisement in one of the National Newspapers for an employment opportunity at Hudson Bay Mining in Flin Flon, Manitoba, Canada.

After successfully passing the interview and immigration processes, along with his wife Helen and daughters Samantha, 7, and Colette, 4, he arrived in Flin Flon in April of 1981 where he took up a position as an industrial mechanic. He obtained Red Seal Interprovincial Industrial Mechanic status by successfully challenging the exam shortly after his arrival. He and his family then quickly settled into the community, purchasing their first home four months after landing in Flin Flon.

As well as industrial mechanics, the mine required several other trades, including electricians, boilermakers, welders, pipefitters and carpenters. Seventy-six families in all arrived to take up residence in the small isolated mining community over the next twelve months. After 36 years of service, when Brian retired, he was the last member of that 1980-81 British invasion to be employed at the company.

As a member of the International Association of Machinists (IAM) 1848, Brian served as branch recording secretary for a number of years. He was promoted to the staff position of Maintenance Health and Safety Co-ordinator in 1989, a position he held until his retirement in 2017. During his 28 years in that position, he served on the company's volunteer Hazmat Team and Fire Department for eight years.

As part of his responsibilities as a safety Co-ordinator, Brian was involved in all aspects of health and safety, which included worker and supervisor training, accident investigation, inspections and audits, working closely with union health and safety committees. He was a member of the Canadian Society of Safety Engineers for over 20 years. Brian also served as a Canadian Registered Safety Professional from April 7, 2000, until his retirement.

Brian now has three grandchildren, Brandon, Keenan, and Kelsey, and four great-grandchildren, Aryna, Addienna, Zavrett, and Benjamin.

Nowadays, Brian has a passion for playing darts, swimming, fishing and travelling the world with Helen, his wife of over 47 years. Since retirement, Brian spends spring summer and fall at their home at Bakers Narrows Provincial Park just outside of Flin Flon. In the winter, he joins other snowbirds in Osoyoos, BC.

Manufactured by Amazon.ca
Bolton, ON